207.1

cr

D0342324

17976

Library
Oakland S.U.M.

Library
Oakland S.U.M.

The
WORLD
on TRIAL

STUDIES IN ROMANS

Other books by Richard W. De Haan

The Living God

Israel and the Nations in Prophecy

227.1
DeH

The WORLD on TRIAL

STUDIES IN ROMANS

Richard W. De Haan

Teacher of the Radio Bible Class

ZONDERVAN PUBLISHING HOUSE
Grand Rapids, Michigan

THE WORLD ON TRIAL
© 1970 by
Zondervan Publishing House
Grand Rapids, Michigan

Library of Congress Catalog Card No. 76-121360

No part of this book may be reproduced in any form
whatever (except for brief quotations in review) without the written permission of the publisher.

Printed in the United States of America

/3∂

Contents

Introduction

The title of this book, *The World on Trial,* expresses the essential and underlying Biblical truth that every moment of every day every human being lives under the scrutiny of God, who is both righteous in His demands and just in His judgments. Since everyone sins, the infinitely holy Judge has declared that all are guilty and deserving of eternal death, which is endless separation from Himself. The book of Romans, which even the most radical critics of the New Testament acknowledge as written by Paul and therefore authentic, begins by presenting the picture of the guilt all men share, and then presents God's answer to man's unhappy predicament.

The theme of Romans is "the gospel of God" (Rom. 1:1), the good news, which has its origin in God, has been foretold in type and promise in the Old Testament, and has been fully revealed in Jesus Christ. This joyful message is inseparable from the person of Christ who was truly man — "made of the seed of David according to the flesh"; but also God — "declared to be the Son of God with power, according to the spirit of holiness, by the resurrection from the dead" (Rom. 1:3). This Gospel of God revealed in Christ is powerful and effective, bringing about the salvation of sinners from the guilt and bondage of sin. The apostle Paul had experienced this power in his own life and had seen it operate in the lives of multitudes, and therefore triumphantly declared,

> For I am not ashamed of the gospel of Christ; for it is the power of God unto salvation to everyone that believeth; to the Jew first, and also to the Greek.
> For in it is the righteousness of God revealed from faith to faith; as it is written, The just shall live by faith (Rom. 1:16, 17).

This good news is also called "the gospel of Christ," for it centers upon the Lord Jesus. The second person of the eternal Trinity became a member of the human race through His virgin birth, lived a life of perfect obedience to God, died a vicarious death upon the cross, conquered death by resurrection, and now has been exalted to the place of highest honor at the right hand of God in Heaven.

The term "salvation" means deliverance from sin — both its guilt and pollution. Any person with a sound mind will admit, in moments of honesty, that if a holy God exists, he stands before this God a guilty sinner. He also must acknowledge that he is unable to be the kind of person he knows he ought to be. Therefore he is in need of two things: forgiveness of his sins and a new power which will enable him to be victorious over the sins to which he is now a slave. This deliverance has been made possible through the work of Jesus Christ, and is available to all who will believe the Gospel.

A proper understanding of what Paul means when he speaks of "the righteousness of God" is also an absolute essential to a comprehension of the Gospel message. This "righteousness of God" is not primarily a reference to one of His divine attributes; that is, the Lord's absolute righteousness which flows necessarily from His holy nature, but to the gift He bestows upon men who believe. Paul, because he was thoroughly versed in the Old Testament Scriptures and the Hebrew faith, did not think of God's righteousness as a moral quality, but as a legal standing. A Jew who was well schooled in the Old Testament defined righteousness as the state of "being right with God," and considered unrighteousness as the state of "being wrong" in relation to God. The Hebrew, therefore, always looked upon himself in all his actions as standing in the presence of God before whom he was "in the right" whenever he acted righteously, and "in the wrong" whenever he sinned; and Paul declares that the Gospel reveals the way by which sinners can be made to stand "in the right" before a holy God. Jesus Christ became man to fulfill the righteous demands of God. He paid the price for human sin. His deity, the glory of which He voluntarily set aside, rendered infinite value to His sacrifice, making it sufficient to pay for the sin of the whole world. God is therefore able to retain His inherent holiness and still forgive guilty sinners.

Christian friend, you may need to come back to these basic truths from time to time. When you become discouraged with yourself, wondering why you haven't progressed farther along the road to practical holiness, and are tempted to doubt your salvation, read again the first chapters of this epistle. You will be reminded of the fact that your salvation is grounded upon what

God has done for you, and not upon your own goodness. You will have imprinted upon your consciousness once again the wonderful truth that God has declared you righteous in Christ on the basis of your faith. You will indeed enter Heaven, not through any works which you have done, but wholly because Jesus Christ earned salvation for you.

An understanding of Romans will also enable you to witness effectively, and to help people who have been deceived by false doctrine. If you comprehend the clear teachings of the first eight chapters of Romans, you will have all the knowledge you need to correct the underlying errors of the cults. Furthermore, having grasped the wonderful truth that God has forgiven your sin, removed you from condemnation, and given you eternal life, you will possess joy, certainty, and victory. Indeed, a serious study of Paul's epistle to the Romans can be a life-transforming experience.

RICHARD W. DeHAAN

Property of
First Assembly of God
Santa Barbara, California

1

Trial of Immoral Pagan

A courtroom scene provides almost unparalleled drama. Major trials sometimes cover weeks or even months of time. The charges and countercharges, the testimonies of many witnesses, the conclusions of experts in various fields, along with exciting cross-examinations combine to keep the spectators in a state of breathless suspense. The attorneys deliver their final pleas and rest their cases. Finally the time has come for the judge to announce the decision. Guilty or not guilty — which will it be? If the verdict is "not guilty" — it's freedom for the defendant; if "guilty" — the penalty must be imposed.

The first three chapters of Romans in many ways may be likened to a courtroom scene. God himself is the Judge. All the people of the world are the defendants. The prosecuting attorney is that able and distinguished scholar who was educated at the feet of Gamaliel — none other than the apostle Paul. The charge against the world is that men are guilty of breaking the law of God, and the death penalty is demanded from every individual.

First of all, mankind is accused of breaking God's law. Secondly, a plea of innocence is entered by the accused, and the arguments raised by the defendants are examined. Thirdly, the evidence of man's guilt is presented to substantiate the charge.

I. THE CHARGE OF GUILT

The declaration that man is guilty before God and deserving of His wrath is clearly and eloquently stated.

> For the wrath of God is revealed from heaven against all ungodliness and unrighteousness of men, who hold the truth in unrighteousness,
> Because that which may be known of God is manifest in them; for God hath shown it unto them (Rom. 1:18, 19).

11

The words "ungodliness and unrighteousness of men" depict man's sinful state. "Ungodliness" indicates his utter disregard of God, his tendency to live as if he were not a morally responsible creature who must someday give an account before a holy God. The second descriptive word, "unrighteousness," refers to wickedness of conduct. It is self-gratification by the most degraded practices, and the serving of self even when it means trampling upon the rights and welfare of other people. Man is *ungodly* in that he does not honor his Creator, and *unrighteous* in his actions toward his fellow men.

Men are not only desperately wicked; they are also responsible for their sad plight. That is why "the wrath of God is revealed from heaven." God is angry with man because of his sin. Yes, even those who have never received special revelation through prophets, visions, or the written Word of God, can observe, if they only will, that sin results in punishment. Furthermore, men "hold the truth in unrighteousness." They suppress the truth, resolutely refusing to acknowledge that they are morally responsible to a holy God. The human race has chosen the path of sin, rejecting both the natural and special revelation of God. Thus, within the compass of one long sentence (Rom. 1:18, 19), man's deplorable condition and unmistakable guilt arc clearly expressed.

II. THE PLEA OF INNOCENCE

The natural man rejects the Biblical picture of himself as a guilty sinner in God's sight. If he believes in a Supreme Being, he thinks of Him as a kind Heavenly Father too merciful to punish sinners. He makes excuses for his sins and claims a right to favor with God because he is living more righteously than many around him. In addition, this self-righteous person enjoys pointing to the pagan world as proof that all men cannot be held guilty in God's sight. He claims that these people are ignorant of God's existence and therefore cannot know His will.

A. *Ignorance of God's Existence*

The heathen nations do not have God's special revelation until the Gospel is proclaimed to them; and therefore some object to the idea that they can be classed as "ungodly." How can they honor a God concerning whom they have never heard?

The answer to this objection is found in the fact of God's general revelation of himself to all men. His power and deity are declared in the universe He created and sustains. All men are responsible, even the pagans, because they have rejected the light God has given them.

> Because that which may be known of God is manifest in them; for God hath shown it unto them.
>
> For the invisible things of him from the creation of the world are clearly seen, being understood by the things that are made, even his eternal power and Godhead, so that they are without excuse (Rom. 1:19, 20).

Yes, every person who possesses some ability to think or reason may know certain truths about God from the world in which he lives. The Psalmist, awed by the living beauty of the oriental sky, sees the heavens as singing a perpetual anthem of glory to God. By day they pour forth their speech like a bubbling fountain, and by night they declare the mysterious and secret knowledge of God.

> The heavens declare the glory of God, and the firmament showeth his handiwork.
>
> Day unto day uttereth speech, and night unto night showeth knowledge (Ps. 19:1, 2).

This anthem of the heavens is more universal than any human language, and therefore can be understood by all men. Israelite or Gentile, black or white, educated or uneducated, wherever the light penetrates and the darkness falls, *the wordless speech of the heavens* declares God's presence and power.

> There is no speech nor language, where their voice is not heard.
>
> Their line is gone out through all the earth, and their words to the end of the world. In them hath he set a tabernacle for the sun,
>
> Which is like a bridegroom coming out of his chamber, and rejoiceth like a strong man to run a race.
>
> His going forth is from the end of the heaven, and his circuit unto the ends of it; and there is nothing hidden from the heat thereof (Ps. 19:3-6).

Any intelligent person who listens to the voice of his heart as he observes the heavens will acknowledge that behind it all is a wise Designer and powerful Creator. The searching soul who begins with this will be led to faith in God.

B. *Ignorance of God's Will*

Many people, while expressing belief in a Supreme Being, are unwilling to accept the idea that He can be known, or His will comprehended. They declare that the things man may learn about God through nature are not enough to make him responsible for his conduct. This assertion does not stand when carefully examined, because in addition to the revelation of God in the universe, every person has an inner consciousness of what is right and wrong. Even though the light of conscience has been dimmed because of deliberate wickedness, it still exists everywhere. At one time all men knew God, but they failed to glorify Him and give Him thanks. They deliberately turned from the light, began to think wrongly and act foolishly, and plunged themselves more deeply into spiritual darkness.

> Because, when they knew God, they glorified him not as God, neither were thankful, but became vain in their imaginations, and their foolish heart was darkened (Rom. 1:21).

Spiritual ignorance is not the *cause* of ungodliness, but its *result*. Men knew God, but they did not properly respond to this knowledge. The plea "not guilty" advanced by the people of the heathen world cannot be justified. God has revealed himself through nature and conscience, but men have rejected both.

III. The Evidence of Blameworthiness

Having asserted that men are guilty before God, and that they have no right to claim innocence because of ignorance, Paul continues by showing how life in his day confirmed his charges. The people of the first century knew that the trend had been to increasing immorality, that living had become empty for many, that the family was no longer a strong social force, and that numerous people were seeking escape through suicide. The apostle Paul pointed to these conditions as proof that the wicked world was and is under God's just condemnation.

A. *The Vanity of Godlessness*

God acts in judgment when men reject Him, "giving them up" to become slaves of their own evil passions.

> Wherefore, God also gave them up to uncleanness through the lusts of their own hearts, to dishonor their own bodies between themselves,
>
> Who exchanged the truth of God for a lie, and worshiped

and served the creature more than the Creator, who is blessed forever. Amen (Rom. 1:24, 25).

Whenever society becomes blatantly godless, its homes begin to crumble, vile homosexual practices become commonplace, and a general spirit of frustration and fear grips the hearts of both youth and adults. People who live wickedly cannot find true pleasure, because God made men to obey Him and honor Him. Whenever they refuse His truth and embrace their own ideas, He gives them over to the control of their evil hearts. Sin begets sin, and continuance in it brings increasing enslavement. This process was apparent at the time Paul wrote his epistle to the Romans, and is certainly evident today. Corruption and anxiety are indications that God has delivered mankind over to the slavery of evil passions.

B. *The Tragedy of Gross Moral Perversion*

When a society deliberately rejects God, He abandons it to moral uncleanness, and its immorality becomes increasingly disgraceful. Men and women turn to the abnormal and unnatural, and the result is reflected in their personalities.

> For this cause God gave them up unto vile affections; for even their women did exchange the natural use for that which is against nature;
> And likewise also the men, leaving the natural use of the woman, burned in their lust one toward another, men with men working that which is unseemly, and receiving in themselves that recompense of their error which was fitting (Rom. 1:26, 27).

Undoubtedly every decent citizen in Rome was revulsed by the gross sexual sins of that day. These evil practices in the past had made Sodom and Canaan a stench in the nostrils of God. No nation has ever remained strong, nor have any people retained moral fiber when these practices became widespread. Mankind today should listen to the voice of history, for it confirms the warning of God's Word. Even as the powerful Roman Empire gradually rotted from within and fell to barbarian invaders, so our Western civilization is headed for destruction unless it changes its present course. We should be alarmed that homosexuality is not even frowned upon in some quarters, and should recognize that it is here as an act of judgment from God, who is giving men up "unto vile affections."

C. *The Insanity of Sin*

Since the pleasures of sin do not provide true and lasting satisfaction, those who live only for the gratification of evil passions experience frustrations and despair. Though sinners may have moments of personal enjoyment, they live under the shadow of certain doom. They delight in drawing others to walk the road to destruction with them, but certainly do not find anything purposeful or real in their human existence. Paul describes the insanity of life dedicated to sin in the following words:

> And even as they did not like to retain God in their knowledge, God gave them over to a reprobate mind, to do those things which are not seemly,
> Being filled with all unrighteousness, fornication, wickedness, covetousness, maliciousness; full of envy, murder, strife, deceit, malignity; whisperers,
> Backbiters, haters of God, insolent, proud, boasters, inventors of evil things, disobedient to parents;
> Without understanding, covenant breakers, without natural affection, implacable, unmerciful;
> Who, knowing the judgment of God, that they who commit such things are worthy of death, not only do the same but have pleasure in them that do them (Rom. 1:28-32).

The history of the human race and the conditions of the world today confirm the truth of Romans 1. Men are depraved and vile sinners, and are responsible for their desperate condition.

Yes, the world of mankind is guilty, even those who have never heard the Gospel of the Lord Jesus Christ. Every person has rejected to some extent the light of God, and is therefore accountable to Him. We need not concern ourselves, however, with theoretical problems that arise in connection with God's final judgment upon those to whom His special revelation never came. We may be certain that He will deal in absolute justice, and that no one will be punished unjustly. The truth for you to consider, my friend, is the fact that you are a sinner by nature and choice, and that you stand before God guilty and deserving of eternal death. The Gospel of Christ is good news for you. It tells you that the same Judge who pronounces the whole world guilty and under condemnation has provided salvation for your sins. He gave His own precious Son, Jesus Christ, to die in your place.

> For God so loved the world, that he gave his only begotten Son, that whosoever believeth in him should not perish, but have everlasting life (John 3:16).

When you trust in the Savior, God declares you justified. He provides a clean slate, a perfect record, so that you who were once guilty, condemned, and without excuse can now stand before Him without blemish. You can be saved today!

> But as many as received him, to them gave he power to become the children of God, even to them that believe on his name (John 1:12).

2

Trial of Self-Righteous Moralist

A study of Romans 1 should convince every person that all men who live in gross immorality are responsible for their conduct and are therefore guilty before God. However, many are willing to agree that those who flaunt the standards of decency deserve God's wrath, but insist that they themselves should not be classed as ungodly and wicked sinners. Some of these self-righteous people are only moderately religious, but they take pride in their rectitude of character. Others are deeply religious, feeling that on this basis they possess a superiority to the rest of mankind. They are smug and self-satisfied, thinking themselves good enough to merit God's favor. The second chapter of Romans shatters the complacency of all who take pride in their own moral goodness.

I. MORAL REALITY DECLARES GUILT

One of the most important functions of the Word of God is to show the self-righteous moralist that he is indeed a guilty sinner, and it accomplishes this end by unmasking his superficial show of righteousness.

The person who looks upon himself as good and worthy of God's approval needs to see that his righteousness is shallow and merely external. He must be made aware of the fact that God knows man's heart, and that even his best deeds are tainted by unworthy motives and selfish pride. Paul therefore declares,

> Therefore, thou art inexcusable, O man, whosoever thou art that judgest; for wherein thou judgest another, thou condemnest thyself; for thou that judgest doest the same things.
>
> But we are sure that the judgment of God is according to truth against them who commit such things.
>
> And thinkest thou this, O man, that judgest them who do such things, and doest the same, that thou shalt escape the judgment of God? (Rom. 2:1-3).

18

The person who is proud of his own morality and piety often sets himself up as a judge of those who are immoral and cruel. If he would only be honest, however, he would soon recognize that he is guilty of the same wrongdoings. He may sin to a lesser degree, and externally appear respectable, decent, and law-abiding. But his motives are often wrong, his attitudes cruel and his thoughts impure. He should realize that God sees his heart, and that His judgment will be according to reality. He should solemnly reflect upon the fact that he will someday stand at God's tribunal, where he will be judged by what he really is, not on the basis of mere external goodness. Any person who accepts this fact will be loathe to criticize others. Instead, he will seek God's forgiveness and ask Him for help.

II. ACCUMULATED EVIL CONFIRMS GUILT

People, living in accordance with the generally accepted moral code of their community and enjoying relative prosperity, often feel that their physical and material blessings are proof that God is pleased with their conduct. They suppose that their comfortable homes, beautiful automobiles, good health, and general popularity are signs of God's pleasure with them. What these outwardly moral and prosperous people fail to recognize, however, is that their good fortune does not necessarily indicate God's approval. Therefore the apostle Paul issues this corrective admonition,

> Or despisest thou the riches of his goodness and forbearance and long-suffering, not knowing that the goodness of God leadeth thee to repentance?
> But after thy hardness and impenitent heart treasurest up unto thyself wrath against the day of wrath and revelation of the righteous judgment of God (Rom. 2:4, 5).

God extends His kindness to men that He might lead them to repentance. Those who live according to their own standards of goodness, thinking their material and physical blessings are indications that God is indifferent to their sins, are grievously mistaken. In fact, their obstinate refusal to submit to the truth of God as revealed in Christ means that they are mountains of guilt in the sight of God. They will receive a just retribution for their sins when they stand in the presence of Christ.

Thousands today reject the testimonies of those who have experienced salvation through faith, and deliberately ignore the witness of those who enjoy personal fellowship with the living Christ.

They repudiate the apostle Paul and his report of a dramatic, life-transforming meeting with the Lord Jesus. They reject the Gospel, resolutely refusing to believe the message of the New Testament. They set up their own standards, and make a great show of living in accordance with them. In reality, however, their rejection of Christ is daily increasing the measure of their guilt before God. One day they will stand exposed to His holy wrath.

III. LIFE-CHOICE ESTABLISHES GUILT

The respectable citizen often finds it difficult to accept the idea that he is a guilty sinner, even though he cannot logically deny it. He finds it most humbling to declare that all his works are worthless for salvation, and then to accept the redemption for which another paid the price. Each person brought face to face with the truth, however, must decide either to accept or reject God's salvation. The life-choice he makes will determine both his destiny and the way he will live the rest of his days upon earth.

Since the natural man has a tendency to think of salvation as earned by works, he finds it difficult to understand the doctrine of grace. Opponents of the Gospel have often declared that salvation by faith alone is both unfair and immoral, for they say it gives people a free license to sin. The apostle Paul anticipated this kind of reasoning, and pointed out that God will judge every person, whether saved or unsaved, "according to his deeds":

> To them who by patient continuance in well-doing seek for glory and honor and immortality, eternal life;
> But unto them that are contentious, and do not obey the truth, but obey unrighteousness, indignation and wrath,
> Tribulation and anguish, upon every soul of man that doeth evil, of the Jew first, and also of the Greek;
> But glory, honor, and peace, to every man that worketh good, to the Jew first, and also to the Greek;
> For there is no respect of persons with God (Rom. 2:7-11).

These verses in no way teach that those who do good will earn salvation through their works, but point out that one's conduct will give outward evidence of the life-choice he has made. Those who reject the Gospel and continue in their self-styled righteousness are actually guilty of the most grievous of all sins — the rejection of God's mercy through Christ. Though they may live outwardly respectable lives before men, God sees their evil thoughts, their selfish motives, and their pride. In His sight they "obey unrighteousness," and therefore daily increase their liability to punishment. On the other hand, people who accept God's message and receive the indwelling Holy Spirit make the correct life-choice. Though they still have faults and may often fail, they have made it clear that they are seeking for "glory and honor and immortality." They have become members of God's family through faith, and will never be condemned. True, they will someday stand at the judgment seat of Christ, but not for punishment. They will appear there to receive their respective degrees of glory.

IV. God's Justice Weighs Guilt

The Biblical teaching that every person must someday stand before God for final judgment, and that the degrees of glory for the saved and degrees of punishment for the unsaved will then be awarded, poses many problems to the natural man. The mere thought that every person who has ever lived will be individually examined is staggering. No finite human can understand how enough knowledge and wisdom will be available to make this final judgment absolutely fair. People on earth are influenced by hereditary and environmental factors over which they have no control, and no two people have precisely the same opportunities or talents. Then, too, many have never even heard the message of Christ, and have no grasp of what the Bible teaches. It seems utterly impossible to measure out to every individual the exact degree of glory or shame God's justice demands. In answer to this problem Paul declares,

> For as many as have sinned without law shall also perish without law; and as many as have sinned in the law shall be judged by the law
> (For not the hearers of the law are just before God, but the doers of the law shall be justified.
> For when the Gentiles, who have not the law, do by nature the things contained in the law, these, having not the law, are a law unto themselves;
> Who show the work of the law written in their hearts, their conscience also bearing witness, and their thoughts the meanwhile accusing or else excusing one another)
> In the day when God shall judge the secrets of men by Jesus Christ according to my gospel (Rom. 2:12-16).

A. *God's Justice Exalted*

The human mind is unable to comprehend fully the greatness

of God's wisdom or the glory of His holiness. No judge or jury has ever been able to administer absolute justice, for no human can infallibly consider all the factors involved. Those who possess faith, however, are confident that the omnipotent and omniscient God who created and sustains the world is able to do so. The declaration of the apostle Paul in these verses may be paraphrased as follows:

> Those who have never been introduced to God, as He is revealed in the sacred Scriptures and through Jesus Christ, will be held responsible only for the revelation accessible to them. They will be judged by the light that was available, and will not be held responsible for truth they never received.
>
> A man is justified in the sight of God not by mere familiarity with God's special revelation but by obedience to it. When heathen people instinctively do right things, they manifest a law within themselves. They demonstrate the effect of such a law working in their own hearts. Conscience responds to this norm or standard. As that inner voice speaks and they reflect upon it, their thoughts either condemn or commend their conduct. We may be sure that God will take all these things into account when He will judge by Jesus Christ even the deepest secrets of men's lives.

B. *God's Justice and You*

To understand God's justice you must acknowledge that you are a sinner and are deserving of punishment at the hands of a holy God. However, it may be that you are sincerely struggling with intellectual problems concerning the Christian faith. Knowing that only a small portion of mankind has ever been introduced to the Gospel, you wonder how God could have been so negligent. You find it difficult to accept the idea that those who do not trust Christ will suffer God's wrath through all eternity. Three things may be said which at least in part will answer the problem you face.

First, we must place the blame where it belongs. Redeemed people have failed, through laziness and indifference, to proclaim the good news to the ends of the earth. On the whole, they also have given a poor demonstration of Christ's presence in their personal lives. In times of persecution and distress the followers of Christ have given striking evidence of His transforming power and sustaining grace, but under more favorable conditions they tend to become worldly, selfish, and complacent. You see, God has commanded saved human beings to be the messengers of the

Gospel, and we have failed. The unsaved multitudes today, whether in areas where the Gospel has never been preached or in the midst of professing believers, are in their sad spiritual plight, not because God has decreed it, but possibly because we who know Him have been inconsistent, unconcerned, and self-centered.

Secondly, we must remember that privilege always increases responsibility. The Lord knows the entire situation and understands that people hear the Gospel in widely differing circumstances. He will be thoroughly just in dealing with all men. Judgment will be meted out on a fair basis.

> But he that knew not, and did commit things worthy of stripes, shall be beaten with few stripes. For unto whomsoever much is given, of him shall be much required; and to whom men have committed much, of him they will ask the more (Luke 12:48).

Thirdly, if a person sincerely desires to know God and follows the light he has received, the Lord will ultimately lead him to salvation. The Ethiopian eunuch was reading Isaiah 53, but couldn't understand it. God sent a missionary in the person of Philip to present Christ to this man. Missionaries have often reported that when they entered territories where the Gospel had never been preached, they found hearts thoroughly prepared for the message of Christ. In one instance a group of people eagerly accepted the Lord, saying, "We have known Him for years, and have worshiped Him, but we never knew His name."

Thinking of the lost and their ultimate punishment, we acknowledge our inability to solve every problem that might be presented. We do not know the exact nature or intensity of the suffering of the condemned, but we do know that the question of Abraham, "Shall not the Judge of all the earth do right?" (Gen. 18:25), is to be answered in the affirmative. Yes, God will be absolutely just!

The important question for you to answer is, "What will God do with me?" You have heard the Gospel. You know you are a sinner, and you have been told that God has provided a remedy for your sin. You must make a life-choice by believing on Jesus Christ, acknowledging Him as your Savior and Lord. He died for your sins on the cross of Calvary, and conquered death for you. He offers *you* salvation as a free gift. The Bible says:

> For by grace are ye saved through faith; and that not of yourselves, it is the gift of God —
> Not of works, lest any man should boast (Eph. 2:8, 9).

3

Trial of Proud Religionist

In this study we will observe the third aspect of the "World on Trial," as it is recorded in Romans 2:17-29. The first phase of the "trial" established the fact that the iniquitous heathen world is guilty and deserving of death (Rom. 1:18-32). The second stage (Rom. 2:1-16) showed the self-righteous moralists, both Jewish and pagan, to be condemned before God also. The lesson before us now deals specifically with proud religionists, people not at all reluctant to look upon the rest of mankind as condemned, but who feel certain of their own favor with God because of their meticulous religionist observances. They proudly assert that because they have the "right religion," they do not share the guilt and condemnation of the masses.

The apostle Paul directly addressed those who were so proud of their religion, saying,

> But if thou art called a Jew, and restest in the law, and makest thy boast of God,
> And knowest his will, and approvest the things that are more excellent, being instructed out the law,
> And art confident that thou thyself art a guide of the blind, a light of them who are in darkness,
> An instructor of the foolish, a teacher of babes, who hast the form of knowledge and of the truth in the law —
> Thou, therefore, who teachest another, teachest thou not thyself? Thou that preachest a man should not steal, dost thou steal? (Rom. 2:17-21).

With these words the apostle indicated these religionists, so signally favored by the Lord, with demanding a standard of conduct from the heathen they themselves did not follow. He proceeded to charge them with breaking three of their own Ten Commandments, and accused them of blaspheming God's name.

24

I. Religious But Guilty of Theft

One of the criticisms often leveled against outwardly pious people is that they observe certain religious regulations and prohibitions, but are careless about their own basic ethical and moral standards. Paul knew this to be true of the people he was addressing, and declared them guilty of breaking the eighth commandment.

> . . . Thou that preachest a man should not steal, dost thou steal? (Rom. 2:21).

Most people resent any implication that they are thieves. The Pharisees, strictly orthodox leaders in Judaism during the apostolic age, became infuriated with Jesus Christ when He strongly denounced them, telling them they were guilty of extorting money from helpless widows while making an outward show of goodness. He had said that they were like the person who carefully washes the outside of the cup and platter, but leaves the inside dirty; that they were outwardly scrupulous, but that they were corrupting themselves by their greed and dishonest practices.

> Woe unto you, scribes and Pharisees, hypocrites! For ye make clean the outside of the cup and of the platter, but within they are full of extortion and excess (Matt. 23:25).

Yes, these pietistic people were indeed guilty of greed, dishonesty, and theft.

Moving forward in history some 1900 years to this present moment, we can declare without fear of contradiction that self-righteous, religious people today are likewise guilty of breaking God's laws, and that they are just as culpable as the people to whom Paul spoke. Perhaps you call yourself a Christian because you attend church faithfully, contribute regularly, and do many good works in the hope they will help earn a place in Heaven for you. You have not really concerned yourself too much about doctrinal matters, and have no clear idea concerning the reason for Christ's death or the reality of His resurrection. In fact, you have looked upon the doctrines of Christianity as quite unimportant, feeling that the crucial matter is your life, not your beliefs. You should realize, however, that you are a sinner, and that you cannot earn your way to Heaven. I would like to have you ask yourself this question, "Have I ever been guilty of dishonesty or theft?" True, you may never have staged a holdup, robbed a bank, or taken money from a cash register. But what about the last income tax report? How about that shady business deal? or that lie you told to obtain a refund from a department store? Don't you think you were stealing when you wasted that time at work? Yes, in one way or another you have been dishonest, you have made yourself guilty, and forfeited the right to Heaven. You are in need of salvation through God's grace and by faith in Christ. You must acknowledge that you are a sinner, believe that Jesus Christ paid the price for your sins, and humbly commit your life to Him.

Even true believers sometimes need to be reminded that they can unwittingly break God's commandments. Some people who scrupulously avoid the worldly practices their church condemns are a displeasure to the Lord because they have a tendency to be greedy or dishonest. Christian friend, if you have allowed greed to control your actions, you must confess your sin and ask God to give you victory. Many unsaved people are kept from Christ because of the inconsistency they see in the lives of believers. Let it not be said of you that you are religious, but guilty of theft.

II. Religious But Guilty of Adultery

Sins of moral impurity, while not uncommon, are always offensive. Most tragic, however, is the fact that even religious people become involved in these practices, not in the open and shameless manner of the atheist or agnostic, but secretly. Their immorality is usually accompanied by an attempt to salve a guilty conscience and justify the deed in the sight of others. Knowing that behind the pious façade of religiosity a great deal of adultery is practiced, Paul asked,

> Thou that sayest a man should not commit adultery, dost thou commit adultery? . . . (Rom. 2:22).

The devout religionists who disliked the apostle Paul and his message may have resented this blunt question. Some of them undoubtedly felt uneasy because they had indeed committed this overt act. Others, though having abstained from the actual practice of sexual immorality, could not claim complete innocence in the light of what Jesus Christ had said.

> Ye have heard that it was said by them of old, Thou shalt not commit adultery;
> But I say unto you that whosoever looketh on a woman to lust after her hath committed adultery with her already in his heart (Matt. 5:27, 28).

These words of the Lord Jesus in no way contradict the Old Testament Scriptures, which clearly declare that sin begins in the heart, and that it consists in more than the outward deed. The writer of Proverbs, warning against an evil woman, wrote,

> Lust not after her beauty *in thine heart* . . . (Prov. 6:25).

When David in sorrow confessed his grave sin with Bathsheba, he admitted that the wicked deed originated within his heart, and prayed,

> Create in me a clean heart, O God, and renew a right spirit within me (Ps. 51:10).

Friend, a self-righteous attitude that considers only the outward appearance keeps multitudes from Christ and salvation even today. Realizing that the lustful look or impure thought is sin, how can you consider yourself good enough for Heaven? You have violated God's demand for absolute purity, and have demonstrated that your inner nature is corrupt. Every evil and illicit thought is sin in God's sight, and He sees the lustful look as adultery. Therefore, who dares claim innocence regarding violation of the seventh commandment?

If you will honestly examine yourself in the light of the Scriptures, your self-righteousness will fly away. You will recognize that you are guilty of sinning against God, that you are justly condemned, and that you need the salvation He provides in grace. You will be willing to receive the gift of eternal life through faith in Jesus Christ.

III. RELIGIOUS BUT GUILTY OF IDOLATRY

The popular conception of idolatry is that it consists in the worship of man-made images, but this is a relatively crude form of the practice engaged in by only a few. Even though many have never bowed before an image, they are nevertheless idolaters. The religious people of the Hebrew faith were certainly free from the taint of pagan image worship, but the apostle Paul implied they were guilty of idolatry when he asked,

> . . . Thou that abhorrest idols, dost thou commit sacrilege? (Rom. 2:22).

This query seemed quite unreasonable on the surface. Surely Paul knew they were not guilty of worshiping images. However, their haughty claim that they could not be charged with this sin was the result of their unwillingness to understand the deeply spiritual nature of God's law. The Holy Spirit had taught the beloved apostle that covetousness is a form of idolatry. Two of Paul's epistles explicitly state that a covetous man is an idolater (Eph. 5:5; Col. 3:5). Covetousness is equated with idolatry because God demands and deserves full obedience. Whenever a person is divided in his loyalty, placing such value upon earthly possessions that they hinder his worship and service of God, he is an idolater. God lays claim to absolute priority, commanding men to worship Him alone and to love Him with all their being.

> Hear, O Israel: The LORD our God is one LORD:
> And thou shalt love the LORD thy God with all thine heart,
> and with all thy soul, and with all thy might (Deut. 6:4, 5).

Not many people today worship idols, but multitudes have gods of pleasure, fame, or material wealth. God requires and deserves the full devotion and love of every heart. The Lord Jesus confirmed the command of Deuteronomy 6 and clearly declared man's responsibility to his Maker when He said,

> And thou shalt love the Lord thy God with all thy heart,
> and with all thy soul, and with all thy mind, and with all thy
> strength: this is the first commandment (Mark 12:30).

To the extent that you are not obeying these words you stand guilty in God's presence. You cannot be truly dedicated to Him and have an inordinate love for the things of this world. You cannot be a servant of God and a slave to earthly pleasures or possessions. Therefore you are guilty of idolatry and stand in need of God's forgiveness.

IV. RELIGIOUS BUT GUILTY OF BLASPHEMY

Well-intentioned people can unknowingly deceive themselves. In the spiritual realm, the very people who are proud of their "rightness of religion" may actually defame God by their conduct. This was true of the orthodox religionists to whom Paul was speaking, for he charged them with being lawbreakers who actually dishonored God's name while professing to love Him.

> Thou that makest thy boast of the law, through breaking the
> law dishonorest thou God? (Rom. 2:23).

The religious leaders of Jewry proudly affirmed a unique relationship to God, but showed little of His purity, goodness and mercy in their lives. The heathen world blasphemed the God of Israel because of what it saw in those who claimed to be His special people. Even the Pharisees, the party most zealously concerned with keeping the law of Moses, were dishonest, cruel, and hypocritical. They brought reproach upon the name of the Lord, and shortly before His crucifixion Christ issued this scathing denunciation of them:

> But woe unto you, scribes and Pharisees, hypocrites! For ye shut up the kingdom of heaven against men; for ye neither go in yourselves, neither permit them that are entering to go in.
> Woe unto you, scribes and Pharisees, hypocrites! For ye devour widows' houses, and for a pretense make long prayers; therefore, ye shall receive the greater damnation.
> Woe unto you, scribes and Pharisees, hypocrites! For ye compass sea and land to make one proselyte, and when he is made, ye make him twofold more the child of hell than yourselves (Matt. 23:13-15).

Let me remind you that even though you are deeply religious, living a moral life, and tenaciously clinging to the historic doctrines of your church, you cannot go to Heaven on the basis of your good works. You may not have committed overt acts of gross sin, but you have entertained evil thoughts of one kind or another. God sees your heart, for "all things are naked and opened unto the eyes of him *with whom we have to do*" (Heb. 4:13). You do not meet the standard required by the infinitely holy God — perfect righteousness of character and conduct. You need to acknowledge that you are a sinner, that you cannot earn salvation, and that your only hope is to receive redemption as a gift from God. You have a choice to make.

> For the wages of sin is death, but the gift of God is eternal life through Jesus Christ, our Lord (Rom. 6:23).

You may choose the wages of sin and eternal separation from God's love and favor, or you may accept the gift of salvation by which He forgives your sins, gives you a new nature, makes you His own child, and guarantees you a place in Heaven. Which do you choose?

4

God's Righteousness Vindicated

The trial of mankind before the tribunal of God is ready to begin its fourth session. The pagans, the moralists, and the proud religionists have been carefully examined and proven guilty and deserving of condemnation. The Scripture for this study, the third chapter of Romans, tells how Paul defends the rightness of God's ways, summarizes His verdict that all men are condemned sinners, and declares God's remedy for the guilt of mankind.

I. THE RIGHTNESS OF GOD'S WAYS DEFENDED

Some Jewish people of Paul's day, who were sincere, religious, and keenly aware of the glory of the Old Testament Scriptures, knew that they were sinners indeed, and that they stood condemned along with pagan and self-righteous moralists. They were perplexed, however, questioning any real advantage in being a member of the nation favored by God with special revelation and a distinct call. Some even felt that God's faithfulness and righteousness were in jeopardy, for He had not fulfilled the promises He gave Israel.

A. *God's Favor Reasserted*

The natural question of any Israelite hearing Paul's declaration that even sincere people with the "right religion" are sinners in need of salvation, is expressed in the first verse of Romans 3.

> What advantage, then, hath the Jew? . . . (Rom. 3:1).

Paul's answer is brief and to the point,

> Much every way, chiefly because unto them were committed the oracles of God (Rom. 3:2).

God had given Israel a verbalized revelation of Himself through the prophets, and this has been preserved in the Old Testament

Scriptures. Since this great advantage belongs to the nation of Israel alone, the Jewish people are assured that it indeed has been a great privilege to be part of the chosen nation.

B. *God's Faithfulness Maintained*

Acknowledging that the Jews enjoyed special privileges, and that being an Israelite was a distinct blessing, a new problem arose in the mind of the questioner. What about God's faithfulness, His dependability to fulfill His promises?

> For what if some did not believe? Shall their unbelief make the faithfulness of God without effect? (Rom. 3:3).

The Israelite asks, "Will God let the unbelief of some make Him a liar?" He has made promises, and He should keep them, regardless of people's unbelief. Paul strongly responds to this argument, saying,

> God forbid: yea, let God be true, but every man a liar; as it is written, That thou mightest be justified in thy sayings, and mightest overcome when thou art judged (Rom. 3:4).

The point Paul is making is that God's judgment upon those who do not believe Him is in reality a testimony to His own faithfulness. God is true to Himself and His Word. Even those who are His favored people must be subject to His impartial justice.

C. *God's Righteousness and Truth Vindicated*

The apostle knows that still another objection will rise in the hearts of some Israelites who cannot understand that mere membership in the nation does not guarantee entrance into Heaven. They question God's righteousness and truth. It seems unfair to them that the Lord should punish sin, for human disobedience has given God an opportunity to demonstrate His righteousness and justice. In that sense, they say, sin is a good thing.

> But if our unrighteousness commend the righteousness of God, what shall we say? Is God unrighteous who taketh vengeance? (I speak as a man.) (Rom. 3:5).

Paul rejects the claim that sin is good because it brought about salvation,

> God forbid; for then how shall God judge the world? (Rom. 3:6).

Since the Lord is the moral Governor of the universe and the Judge of all the earth, He cannot fulfill His role unless He righteously punishes sin. To make God a partner in sin would be to disqualify Him as a righteous Judge. If this were done, the moral order of the entire world would be destroyed. Without God there would be no law, no order, no purpose, and no hope.

Still another objection is raised against Paul's claim that orthodox religious people are sinners. Why should they need salvation like everyone else? Their proper religion should be enough to maintain them in God's favor, they feel, even though it is true they have sinned in many ways. They raise this objection,

> For if the truth of God hath more abounded through my lie unto his glory, why yet am I also judged as a sinner,
> And not rather (as we are slanderously reported, and as some affirm that we say), Let us do evil, that good may come? Whose condemnation is just (Rom. 3:7, 8).

In these words the claim is made that the truth of God is exalted when contrasted to human falsehood, and that every sin man commits will be worked by God into the fabric of the universe and brought to ultimate good. It certainly wouldn't be right for God to condemn a man for that!

Paul answers with indignation, disturbed that some of his opponents are misrepresenting him. The parenthetical words, "As we are slanderously reported, and as some affirm that we say," are a denial that he has encouraged men to commit evil that good may eventually result. He states that those who circulate this slanderous report deserve to be punished — "whose condemnation is just." Paul thus certifies that God never breaks His word, always judges men fairly, and does not need human sin to demonstrate His attributes. True, God permitted sin to enter His universe, and He will bring about ultimate good. Men must never make this fact an excuse for sin, however, nor see in it a denial of God's faithfulness, righteousness, and truthfulness. The Lord in matchless grace has provided a way of redemption from sin, and in His infinite wisdom He is able to direct even the willful and disobedient acts of His rebellious subjects so that His own eternal plans and purposes are accomplished. Nevertheless, let it be clearly understood that God has always hated sin, and He always will.

The belief that sin is good can stem only from an evil and insensitive soul. You might as well say it is good to break the heart of one who loves you so that he might have a better chance to show his love.

II. The Verdict Repeated

The religious Jew, realizing that Israel has enjoyed great privileges and sinned against more light than the Gentiles, now wonders if Hebrews are actually less favored than the pagan world. The question is raised, "Are we excelled by them?" In other words, "Are we in a worse position than those who have never received God's special message?" (The King James Version raises this question, "Are we better than they?" But the passive form of the verb here in Romans 3:9 suggests the translation, "Are we excelled by them?") Paul's answer is a resounding

> . . . No, in no way; for we have before proved both Jews and Greeks, that they are all under sin (Rom. 3:9).

Privileged or not privileged, Jews and Gentiles in their standing before God are equally in need of divine grace. No one can redeem himself by his own efforts.

In the verses that follow (Rom. 3:10-18), Paul refers to six Old Testament quotations summarizing the sinfulness of man before a God who is Judge, Physician and Historian.

A. *Man's Guilt*

Reviewing the truth that all men are guilty, Paul portrays God as Judge looking down upon the human race and pronouncing that no one is righteous or truly seeking after Him. All fail to honor Him, and it is impossible to find anyone whose works are perfect.

> As it is written, There is none righteous, no, not one:
> There is none that understandeth, there is none that seeketh after God.
> They are all gone out of the way, they are together become unprofitable; there is none that doeth good, no, not one (Rom. 3:10-12).

B. *Man's Spiritual Sickness*

God is then pictured as the all-seeing Physician who describes the human race in its foulness, deceitfulness, maliciousness, vindictiveness, and cruelty.

Their throat is an open sepulcher; with their tongues they
have used deceit; the poison of asps is under their lips;
Whose mouth is full of cursing and bitterness.
Their feet are swift to shed blood (Rom. 3:13-15).

C. *Man's Dismal Failure*

Finally, God is presented as the One who knows all history,
declaring the human race a miserable failure because it has never
fulfilled the purpose for which it was made. Instead, strife and
wickedness have been the concomitants of man's existence.

Destruction and misery are in their ways;
And the way of peace have they not known.
There is no fear of God before their eyes (Rom. 3:16-18).

Following this convincing summary of human iniquity, Paul draws
his conclusion.

Now we know that whatever things the law saith, it saith
to them who are under the law, that every mouth may be
stopped, and all the world may become guilty before God
(Rom. 3:19).

The word "law" undoubtedly refers to the various quotations
Paul has just made from the Old Testament. Since one came
from Isaiah and the remainder from the Psalms, Paul is not speaking expressly of the Mosaic Law, the legal code God gave to
Israel alone. The eternal principles of right and wrong found in
the law of Moses are repeated throughout the Old Testament,
however, and are applicable to all men. Every person, Jew or
Gentile, is guilty before God when he does not truly seek the
Lord, practices deceit, acts maliciously, and manifests vindictiveness and cruelty. The apostle declares, therefore, that he has
quoted these Scriptures that "Every mouth may be stopped, and
all the world may become guilty before God." He has brought
all mankind before the divine judgment bar, and declared them
guilty. The evidence of history, the testimony of their own lives,
and the witness of Scripture silences the lips of all. No man with
any degree of truthfulness and sincerity could deny his own basic
wickedness. No one with any respect for the laws of logic could
claim that God has no right to condemn such sinners.

It is impossible for fallen man to render perfect obedience to
God, and therefore salvation cannot be earned. Whoever seeks
to do so in his own strength will surely fail.

> Therefore, by the deeds of the law there shall no flesh be
> justified in his sight; for by the law is the knowledge of sin
> (Rom. 3:20).

While it is true that God's standard is perfect, and that obedience
to it would secure divine blessing, the fact remains that in actual
life no one is able to keep it. The law imparts the knowledge of
sin, and enables the sinner to perceive that through the works of
the law no person will be justified. Paul uses the term "no flesh"
instead of "no person" to suggest the idea of man in his moral
weakness and corruption. The law of God, whether conceived of
as the Mosaic system, the whole Old Testament, or the universal
consciousness of right and wrong, cannot remove man's guilt. It
can only show men the gravity of their sin and point to the true
remedy. Salvation is received exclusively by personal faith in
Jesus Christ.

III. THE REMEDY ANNOUNCED

Paul has established his case. All mankind is guilty, without
excuse, and under the sentence of God's wrath. Neither is man
able to save himself. However, he need not despair. God has
provided a way by which He can retain His own righteousness
and yet acquit guilty sinners. So vital is this truth, that the apostle
presses into service the language of the law court, the slave
market, and the temple to make it clear.

A. *The Law Court — Justification*

Paul begins to expound upon God's remedy for human sin with
an amazing announcement:

> But now the righteousness of God apart from the law is
> manifested, being witnessed by the law and the prophets,
> Even the righteousness of God which is by faith of Jesus
> Christ unto all and upon all them that believe; for there is
> no difference.
> For all have sinned, and come short of the glory of God,
> Being justified freely by his grace through the redemption
> that is in Christ Jesus (Rom. 3:21-24).

God treats justly condemned sinners as if they were not guilty.
The word translated "justified" is a legal term meaning "to account as righteous," and the word translated "freely" means "as
a gift." How can God treat bad men as if they were good or

reckon guilty men to be not guilty? How can he give righteousness to men in exchange for simple faith? This seems too good to be true! Furthermore, how can a holy God, the righteous Judge, do that which only a wicked arbiter on earth would do? If it is wrong for human judges to declare guilty men innocent, how can a holy God do so? Isn't it always wrong to declare a sinful man innocent?

B. *The Slave Market — Redemption*

Paul does not immediately answer the question raised concerning the propriety of God's action in acquitting sinners. Instead, he makes a second startling statement,

> Being justified freely by his grace through the redemption that is in Christ Jesus (Rom. 3:24).

God has provided deliverance from the burden of sin through the payment of a price. The Greek word translated "redemption" is *apolutrosis*, and it originally meant "the buying back of a slave or captive." Thus, guilty sinners are informed that Jesus Christ has purchased their redemption from sin and death.

They still do not know to whom Jesus paid the price, however, nor do they understand how God is able to retain His righteousness while declaring sinners guiltless. They are not yet aware of the basis on which God is able to do this.

C. *The Temple Service — Propitiation*

In order to explain these unresolved problems in the minds of his readers, Paul refers to the Temple and its service. Christians, whether brought up as Jews or pagans, are acquainted with various kinds of ritual in connection with sacrifices and offerings. Therefore, they are able to grasp what Paul is saying when he speaks of "propitiation" through the death of Jesus Christ.

> Whom God hath set forth to be a propitiation through faith in his blood, to declare his righteousness for the remission of sins that are past, through the forbearance of God;
> To declare, I say, at this time his righteousness, that he might be just, and the justifier of him who believeth in Jesus (Rom. 3:25, 26).

The key word of these verses is "propitiation" (Greek — *hilasterion*). To the Jewish audience it immediately brings to mind the mercy seat in the holy of holies, where blood was sprinkled annually by the high priest to cover the sins of the nation. Pagans, having a different concept of deity and forgiveness, would understand this word to speak of placating or appeasing the gods. Therefore, both Jews and Gentiles can perceive that the death of Jesus Christ is the means by which God removes sin's guilt. Man's sin exposes him to the wrath of God, which, according to Romans 1:18, "is revealed from heaven against all ungodliness and unrighteousness of men." However, Jesus Christ has borne the punishment all men deserve, for God's wrath against sin fell on Him. God can therefore justly treat guilty sinners as if they were innocent.

Paul goes on to explain that the redemption accomplished by Jesus Christ has retrospective as well as future efficacy. Through the cross, men of faith were saved in the centuries before Christ, as well as those in the years that followed His earthly ministry. His death demonstrates that God was not unrighteous when in Old Testament days He passed over sins. In the self-offering of Christ, God's own righteousness is vindicated and the believing sinner is justified. The Lord, as the representative Man, our substitute, absorbed the punishment incurred by human sin. As God, He gave infinite value to this single sacrifice of Himself, so that it is sufficient to secure forgiveness for all who will believe on Him.

Dear friend, you have been on trial, for you are a sinner by nature and by choice. Do not underestimate your sin. Acknowledge that you are indeed deserving of eternal death. But you must not despair by failing to recognize the great redeeming power of Jesus Christ. You are not too bad to be saved. When William Jay was an old man he said, "My memory is failing, but there are two things I can never forget — that I am a great sinner, and that Jesus Christ is the great Savior." The Lord Jesus has paid the price for your sin in full. There is nothing left for you to do except trust Him. Receive Him today.

> For whosoever shall call upon the name of the Lord shall be saved (Rom. 10:13).

5

Becoming Right With God

Many people look upon faith in God as an unnecessary option. They note the advances in the physical sciences which are taking place with breathtaking swiftness. The marvels of computers and the wonder of space travel excite the imagination of millions. Heart transplants and use of artificial organs, along with other breakthroughs in medical research, hold out to man the promise of a longer lifespan. Some biologists talk excitedly about discovering the secret of life, or suggest that the time is near when parents will be able to determine in advance not only the sex, but also the mental and psychological characteristics of the children they plan to bring into the world. They speak glowingly of the time when man will not be subject to the control of anything outside of himself.

Second thoughts about these scientific claims bring to mind serious problems, however, and many people are deeply disturbed. Man's moral character is such that he cannot be trusted with nuclear weapons, much less control of genetics. In spite of some advances in social concepts, humans today are just as selfish and cruel as their ancestors. Irrational criminal acts make daily headlines, and on every hand is evidence of irresponsible conduct. Therefore, a consideration of man in his relationship to God is not out of place at all; and the subject of this study is, "Becoming Right With God."

No one can predict the degree of success man will achieve in space travel, biology, and medical science, but one can affirm with absolute certainty that he will continue to be sinful, and remain distinctly human. As far back as man's history can be traced in the Bible or archaeology, he has always possessed the faculty of moral judgment, a longing for beauty, and a passion for understanding the real meaning of life. Some fossilized remains of humans indicate that from the dawn of human history man buried his dead in a special way, using flower petals. No animal has ever done this. Furthermore, drawings in caves, considered by some experts to go back thousands of years, reveal that man then, as now, had thoughts about God and eternity. In short, man always has and always will think about himself, and continually seeks to answer the problems of who he is, why he is here, and what awaits him after death. Therefore, the human race will never escape its need of God. Man will never achieve true happiness and inner peace until he has been made right with God. Nothing short of genuine assurance of forgiveness and the joy of real fellowship with the Lord can remove the deep despair and utter loneliness plaguing man today.

This study, focusing upon the fourth chapter of Paul's letter to the Christians in Rome, reveals how God has made provision for man's deep need for fellowship. As you consider this Bible passage, bear in mind that it was written about A.D. 55 by the apostle Paul, a man personally acquainted with many who had talked with Jesus Christ both before and after His resurrection. He himself had been a violent opponent of the Christian message, even approving the death of a young Christian martyr named Stephen. However, one day Paul met Christ and was conquered. His life was transformed, and he became the greatest missionary and apologist of the early church. Though hated, persecuted, often imprisoned, and subjected to many indignities, he unceasingly proclaimed his faith in Jesus Christ until his martyrdom. So, apart from the fact that Paul wrote these words by inspiration, this makes his writings both believable and authoritative for honest seekers after truth. (In fact, a new generation of European scholars is affirming today that we have good reason to believe what Paul says, even when he speaks of miracles and declares that Jesus Christ arose from the dead. How encouraging to see that some who may not believe in verbal inspiration as we do, nevertheless recognize the reliability of Paul's epistles.) Since the authenticity of the apostle's writings is being increasingly certified, no person, not even an unbeliever, should shrug off what they say. Furthermore, the apostle does not deal with interesting but insignificant speculative theories; he writes about *your* relationship with God, which is life's most important issue. His epistles portray man as he really is. They reveal man's selfishness, pride, cruelty, weakness, and estrangement from God. However, they also maintain that he is a moral creature designed by his Maker to exercise dominion over his environment, to enjoy fellowship with God, and to experience satisfying companionship with others in family and social relationships. They show how he can be brought into a right relationship with God through faith in Jesus Christ, and how this will in turn enable him to live in true freedom and genuine happiness. Friend, if you are not "right with God," you are in a state of alienation from Him, and that is why you have worries, fears, and sometimes a deep sense of loneliness. Jesus Christ came into this world and died an ignominious death on the cross to bring you back to God.

I. WHAT IT MEANS TO BE RIGHT WITH GOD

In the fourth chapter of Romans, Paul discusses Abraham, a man honored today by Jews, Moslems and Christians. Though at one time considered by many unbelievers to be a mythical character, he is now recognized by them as a real, flesh-and-blood individual who lived in the Middle East about 4,000 years ago. Abraham spent his youth in Ur, the powerful and prosperous capital of Chaldea. From here he moved to Haran. Both cities were centers for the worship of the moon god Nannar. Abraham was likely an affluent citizen in this highly developed civilization when God called him to begin a new life as a herdsman in Canaan. Without knowing what would be his exact destination, he obeyed God's call as recorded in Genesis 12, and in the following years continued to trust Him despite many discouraging circumstances. God had promised Abraham a son, but his wife Sarah remained barren. Finally, God worked miraculously in the bodies of both Abraham and Sarah, and Isaac was born when both were more than ninety years of age. In spite of sins and imperfections in his life, Abraham was a man of God, knowing Him, loving Him, and walking in fellowship with Him. He was given the distinctive title "Friend of God" (Jas. 2:23).

Abraham, like all other humans was not perfect. The Bible record shows him guilty of lying on two occasions, and indicates that he did not do right when he took Hagar as his concubine (Gen. 16). Since Abraham was guilty of sin, how can we say he was right with God? Is not sin the cause of man's alienation from God? Yes indeed, sin does bring about this estrangement, and, since every person on earth is a sinner, it would seem that no one could ever be right with God. However, the amazing thing about God in His relationship to man is that He treats guilty people as if they were innocent. This is exactly what the Lord did in respect to Abraham.

> For what saith the scripture? Abraham believed God, and
> it was counted unto him for righteousness (Rom. 4:3).

The verb translated "counted" means "to put to one's account."
God in His incredible mercy treats a sinner as if he were a
perfect man. He can do this only because Jesus Christ paid the
price for sin. Paul had explained this in the third chapter when
he said,

> Being justified freely by his grace through the redemption
> that is in Christ Jesus,
> Whom God hath set forth to be a propitiation through faith
> in his blood, to declare his righteousness for the remission of
> sins that are past, through the forbearance of God;
> To declare, I say, at this time his righteousness, that he
> might be just, and the justifier of him who believeth in Jesus
> (Rom. 3:24-26).

Paul spoke of Jesus Christ as the "propitiation," a term which
had meaning for both the Jews and the Greeks to whom he was
writing. The Jewish people were familiar with the Ark of God,
located in the holiest part of the Jewish Temple. The lid of the
Ark was called the "mercy seat," and blood was sprinkled on it
once a year by the high priest. The purpose of the ceremony
was to "cover" the sins of the nation, a concept parallel to that
of propitiation. The pagans, having a different idea of God and
forgiveness, nevertheless offered ritualistic sacrifices to placate or
appease their gods. Both groups, therefore, understood what Paul
meant when he spoke of propitiation.

The death of Jesus Christ is the means by which God removes
the guilt of sin. Man's sin exposes him to the wrath of God,
which, according to Romans 1:18, "is revealed from heaven
against all ungodliness and unrighteousness of men." Jesus Christ
on Calvary has borne the punishment men deserve, however, for
God's wrath against sin fell on Him. God can therefore justly declare guilty sinners innocent. Paul says that the redemption accomplished by the Lord Jesus on the cross paid for the sins of Old
Testament saints as well as future generations, for it was to "declare his righteousness for the remission of sins that are past,
through the forbearance of God" (Rom. 3:25). The Lord could
treat Abraham as if he were sinless on the basis of His knowledge
that Jesus Christ would pay the price for sin in full. To be right
with God, therefore, means that He has graciously removed the
guilt of sin, granted pardon, and then put perfect righteousness to

the sinner's account. Sin is forgiven, alienation is brought to an end, and God is able to adjudge the ungodly person perfectly holy and righteous.

II. HOW TO BECOME RIGHT WITH GOD

The apostle Paul declares explicitly that Abraham became right with God through faith.

> . . . Abraham believed God, and it was counted unto him for righteousness (Rom. 4:3).

In order to properly explain this verse we will first of all carefully define what faith is, and then speak of its exclusiveness.

A. *The Definition of Faith*

Faith is, basically, believing God. It is taking Him at His word. Jesus said, "And ye shall know the truth, and the truth shall make you free" (John 8:32). One cannot intelligently trust the Lord if he knows nothing about Him. He may have true faith even though his understanding is limited, but the Word of God makes it clear that a person is responsible to believe that which God has revealed concerning His character and purposes. The New Testament clearly presents Jesus Christ as the incarnate Son of God who died for sinners, conquered death by resurrection, ascended to Heaven, and is coming again. One may receive Jesus Christ and be made right with God while possessing a limited understanding of His person and work, but no one with true faith will consciously deny the full truth when he understands it. Then, acknowledging his own sinfulness and need of salvation he must personally place his trust in Jesus Christ.

Faith gives the assurance that God's promises will be realized, and that the things we cannot see with the physical eye, or test in the laboratory, are realities more wonderful than the things of this temporal world.

> Now faith is the substance of things hoped for, the evidence of things not seen (Heb. 11:1).

Furthermore, Romans 4:17-21 depicts what Abraham's faith did for him. He was able to believe God even after it was impossible for Sarah and him to have a son. Paul tells us,

> He staggered not at the promise of God through unbelief, but was strong in faith, giving glory to God,

> And being fully persuaded that, what he had promised, he was able also to perform (Rom. 4:20, 21).

Perhaps you find yourself thinking that you could never possess faith like Abraham's. You may feel your own attainment of this faith to be hopeless. Let me assure you, however, that Abraham was right with God long before his faith reached this kind of maturity. Weakness of faith was evidenced on two occasions: when he lied concerning his wife in Egypt, and when he took Hagar as his concubine. These sins and lapses of faith took place in the life of Abraham after the declaration of Genesis 15:6,

> And he believed in the LORD; and he counted it to him for righteousness (Gen. 15:6).

The *degree* of one's faith does not determine his proper relationship to God, but rather the *fact* of this faith. One is not saved by trusting in his own faith. Of utmost importance is *what* you believe, and *in whom* your faith is placed. Even the weakest faith is mighty when its object is great. You may feel your faith is small at times, but remember, faith is only the means by which you appropriate the salvation God has provided, the line that connects you with Jesus Christ. All the benefits of His atoning death and resurrection are yours because your faith, feeble as it may be, is placed in the omnipotent Son of God. If you sincerely believe the verdict of Scripture, which declares you a guilty sinner in God's sight, and truly believe that Jesus Christ as your substitute paid the price for your sin on Calvary, you are a child of God. You have been made right with Him. However, your faith can grow until it becomes an effective power in your life.

B. *The Exclusiveness of Faith*

Since faith by its very nature is implicit personal trust in God and what He has done for our salvation, it excludes all human endeavor as a means of becoming right with God. Works and efforts to keep the law make no contribution. Faith alone is the way. Therefore Paul said,

> Now to him that worketh is the reward not reckoned of grace, but of debt.
> But to him that worketh not, but believeth on him that justifieth the ungodly, his faith is counted for righteousness (Rom. 4:4, 5).

He goes on to declare,

> For the promise that he should be the heir of the world
> was not to Abraham, or to his seed, through the law, but
> through the righteousness of faith.
> For if they who are of the law be heirs, faith is made void,
> and the promise made of no effect,
> Because the law worketh wrath; for where no law is, there
> is no transgression (Rom. 4:13-15).

Moreover, rituals and ordinances or sacraments play no part in
securing salvation. Paul points out that Abraham was made right
with God before he was circumcised. That ceremony came later
as a token of his faith, but not as a means of his reconciliation
with God.

> And he received the sign of circumcision, a seal of the right-
> eousness of the faith which he had yet being uncircumcised . . .
> (Rom. 4:11).

Friend, are you worried, fearful, and lonely? Do you sometimes
feel a deep sense of despair because your life appears to have no
meaning, purpose or goal? If this is a picture of you, let me point
you to Jesus Christ. He came into this world, took upon Himself
our humanity, was delivered to the death of the cross because of
our sins, and rose again to bring about our complete salvation.
He died for you. He was raised from the dead, and, as the living
Christ, He invites you to trust Him. Acknowledge your sinful
condition, your complete and total inability to save yourself,
and believe on the Lord Jesus. God will forgive your sins and remove your guilt. He will receive you as His child, and make
you an heir of eternal glory with Jesus Christ. He will give your
life new meaning and fill you with joyous anticipation.

> That if thou shalt confess with thy mouth the Lord Jesus,
> and shalt believe in thine heart that God hath raised him from
> the dead, thou shalt be saved.
> For with the heart man believeth unto righteousness; and
> with the mouth confession is made unto salvation (Rom. 10:
> 9, 10).

6

Being Right With God

One who reads extensively cannot help but notice that non-Christian literature is largely pessimistic, while optimism characterizes the writings of those who have been made right with God. The well-known atheist, the late Bertrand Russell, writes of "the slow, sure doom falling pitilessly and dark" on us all. The words "anxiety," "absurdity," "alienation," "frustration," "loneliness" and "despair" are constantly repeated by men without God as they describe life. The black cloud of doom that hangs over the horizon in the minds of unbelievers is one reason so many books and magazines today feature adultery, fornication, perversion, sadism, and brutality. Christians, on the other hand, use terms like "faith," "hope," "love," "joy," "certainty," "forgiveness," "fulfillment," and "fellowship" to depict human life.

This striking difference stems from the fact that those who have been made right with God through Jesus Christ have found the answer to their deepest needs. They know that man is more than an accident in nature, a tiny gear in the cosmic mechanism. They recognize man as a rational being who can scientifically investigate and reflect upon the universe in which he lives, and a moral creature longing for beauty and eternal significance who is constantly confronted with decisions regarding right and wrong. They know man is sinful, but believe God has provided a way by which life can be filled with love and hope. On the other hand, the person who holds to the atheistic or mechanistic theory of the universe cannot explain himself, nor can he consistently carry into practice his idea that all of life is nothing.

The sharp contrast between the believer's outlook and that of the naturalist is graphically set forth in Romans 5, where Paul describes the glorious results of being right with God.

I. PEACE WITH GOD — A NEW STANDING

The person who has received Jesus Christ as Savior is at peace with God. Paul declares,

> Therefore, being justified by faith, we have peace with God through our Lord Jesus Christ (Rom. 5:1).

The oldest manuscripts read, "Let us have peace with God," and this is perhaps the most accurate translation. However, it does not mean, "Let us make peace with God," but rather, "Let us enjoy the peace with God which is ours through Jesus Christ." J. B. Phillips accurately translates the verse, "Let us grasp the fact that we have peace with God." This peace is not a subjective feeling, but an objective fact. Man as a sinner outside of Jesus Christ is estranged from God, is hostile to Him, and abides under His wrath, but God sent His Son into the world to make possible a change in the relationship between man and his Maker. Jesus Christ died to redeem us from our sins. God, who is spotlessly pure and infinitely holy, must demand that men do right. When they do wrong He must deal justly, which means punishing them. A good parent cannot declare to his children the necessary rules for proper conduct, prescribe the just penalty for disobedience, and then fail to carry out his word when the rules are broken. Neither can God. For this reason Jesus Christ, the eternal Son, took upon Himself our humanity, lived a perfect life, and died on the cross as our substitute. As a result, God can justly forgive and bring into fellowship with Himself all who will acknowledge their sinfulness, admit their liability to punishment, and by an act of faith receive Jesus Christ.

Paul goes on to describe the new position of the believer.

> By whom also we have access by faith into this grace in which we stand, and rejoice in hope of the glory of God (Rom. 5:2).

The Greek word translated "we have" literally means "we have obtained." The word rendered "access" was used to describe the ushering of a person into the presence of royalty. The French word *entrée* expresses the idea beautifully. The words "this grace" have reference to the new position of divine favor and should be rendered "this state of grace." "We stand" is the translation of the Greek word *estekamen,* and literally means "we stand fast or firm." This verse pictures the fact that when a person believes on the Lord Jesus, the Savior ushers him into the presence of God. The full meaning of Paul's thought may be stated as follows, "Though we deserve wrath and exclusion from God's presence, in Jesus Christ we have gained our entrée to divine favor, where we stand firm."

This truth is of tremendous importance, and many people are confused and defeated in their Christian lives because they do not comprehend it. The Bible teaches that one who receives Christ is justified or declared righteous, and thereby given perfect position or standing. God has declared him righteous and brought him into the place of divine favor. This takes place at the moment a person receives Christ, and needs never to be repeated. This standing in the place of grace and favor is permanent and unaffected by anything the believer might do. Even when a Christian sins he does not lose his position, which God has given him once for all. The joy of his *communion* with Christ will be lost, but not *union* with Him, for that cannot be changed. Confession of sin is the means of restoration to the place of fellowship.

> If we confess our sins, he is faithful and just to forgive us our sins, and to cleanse us from all unrighteousness (I John 1: 9).

Remember, however, that the believer has never lost his standing as a child of God. During the whole cycle of sin, confession, and restoration, his position remains secure.

This truth brings great comfort to the believer. It assures him that he will never lose his salvation. Some may object, feeling that this doctrine leads to carelessness in the Christian life, but this is just not true. The person who has made profession of faith, and then falls away, was never truly justified. The genuine believer will obey God because he loves Him, and, if he persists in sin, he will be chastened by his Heavenly Father. The writer of Hebrews assures us,

> For whom the Lord loveth he chasteneth, and scourgeth every son whom he receiveth (Heb. 12:6).

Christians may rest assured that they can never lose their standing in Christ.

II. HOPE OF GLORY — A NEW EXPERIENCE

God expects believers to have spiritual victories. This was demonstrated by the early Christians who rejoiced in the midst of persecution, certain that even as Jesus Christ conquered death by resurrection and entered into glory, so they too would overcome and share Heaven with Him. True, at some stages in church history Christians displayed an austerity which dimmed the radiance that should have been theirs. Therefore, some people have mistakenly concluded that submitting to the claims of Christ makes for a dull existence, to be endured only because it leads to Heaven in the end. A poet, completely misunderstanding Jesus Christ, said, "Pale Galilean, Thou hast conquered. And the world has grown gray at Thy birth." How utterly wrong these ideas are! Jesus Christ came into the world that men might find true happiness. Angels rejoiced at His birth, and His words and works brought healing and hope to multitudes. After His death, resurrection, and ascension to Heaven, His followers went everywhere proclaiming His redeeming work, demonstrating in their lives His transforming power. Bitter opposition and cruel persecution only intensified their enthusiasm and increased their joyful testimony. Paul accurately described these early Christians when he declared that all who are right with God rejoice in the hope of His glory. For them the resurrection of Jesus Christ was not a vague historical event, but a glorious truth with which they had firsthand acquaintance.

However, the apostle Paul knew that many believers would experience much suffering before entering Heaven. He therefore pointed out three wonderful truths regarding the hope of glory possessed by the followers of Christ. In the first place, Christian joy is to be strengthened through affliction. Secondly, it is based upon God's demonstration of love in Jesus Christ, and does not rest upon mere wishful thinking. Thirdly, the Christian's joyous hope of glory is guaranteed by his union with the living Christ.

A. *Through Present Affliction*

Paul declares that Christians rejoice even in the midst of affliction. He says,

> And not only so, but we glory in tribulations also, knowing that tribulation worketh patience;
> And patience, experience; and experience, hope;
> And hope maketh not ashamed, because the love of God is shed abroad in our hearts by the Holy Spirit who is given unto us (Rom. 5:3-5).

The Greek word translated "tribulation" literally means "pressure." Believers may be subjected to the pressures of poverty, sorrow, persecution, pain, and loneliness. God does not make a cosmic pet out of a person the moment he becomes a Christian. This kind of treatment would neither strengthen his faith nor develop his character. Moreover, people might profess Christ not for salvation from sin but to obtain earthly and material advantages. Suffering, therefore, is an integral part of the believer's life. But, instead of viewing difficult experiences as indications of God's disfavor, Christians are to rejoice in them, because potentially they will produce spiritual gain. The apostle lists three stages of spiritual development attained through suffering: patience, experience, and hope.

1. Patience

The first assertion is that suffering brings patience. The word used is *hupomone,* which does not mean mere passive endurance. It portrays instead the attitude of mind which actively overcomes and conquers the trials of life, the quality that enabled Paul and Silas to sing praises while confined in prison, their feet held by stocks, and their backs bruised and bleeding. This same fortitude was displayed by the early Christians thrown before the wild beasts in the arena. The persecutors saw more than merely the numb silence of victims determined to stoically accept the inevitable. Observers of these early believers saw a radiant optimism in the face of certain death by cruel torture, and many were led to commit themselves to Jesus Christ through this testimony.

2. Experience

Paul goes on to say that tribulation for the Christian results in experience.

> . . . tribulation worketh patience;
> And patience, experience . . . (Rom. 5:3, 4).

The word translated "experience" is often used to describe metal which has passed through the fire so that every impurity has been removed. It has a meaning similar to our use of the word "sterling." The person who meets the pressures of life in the spirit of joyous Christian serenity emerges from the struggle strong and pure.

3. Hope

The third step of a Christian's development through suffering is hope. This strengthening of character makes it possible for him to possess a more vigorous faith as he looks to the future.

> . . . tribulation worketh patience;
> And patience, experience; and experience, hope (Rom. 5:
> 3, 4).

Early believers regarded afflictions not only as an inevitable feature of life, but also as a token of their salvation, "rejoicing that they were counted worthy to suffer shame for his name" (Acts 5:41). Even today the children of God who have gone through the pressures of life in a spirit of joyous confidence have developed true Christian character, and have learned to rejoice in their hope of glory.

Christian, you need not allow life's trials to defeat you. God intends them to lead you to spiritual victory. But you must first take the proper attitude toward the difficulties you experience. If you rebel against them, you will hurt yourself. If you stoically endure them, you will be joyless and gain no benefit from them. See them as the means by which you can become a stronger, better, and purer person, and you will be lifted to a new plateau of spiritual victory. This is true "because the love of God is shed abroad in our hearts by the Holy Spirit who is given unto us" (Rom. 5:5). God imparts the consciousness of His love to those who truly trust Him. Friend, you may be suffering from an incurable disease, your body tortured with pain, and your mind confused as you think of leaving those you love, but you can be assured that God loves you. If you will look at your situation from the perspective of eternity, you will find sweet peace in the assurance that you are now, and always will be, the object of His love and tender care.

B. *Based upon God's Demonstration of Love*

The conviction of God's love and the resultant hope of believers are not merely subjective feelings. They are Christian graces, solidly grounded in the fact that God has supremely demonstrated His love in the death of Jesus Christ on the cross of Calvary. This is the greatest proof of divine love, and has no counterpart. Therefore Paul declares,

> For when we were yet without strength, in due time Christ died for the ungodly.
> For scarcely for a righteous man will one die; yet perhaps for a good man some would even dare to die.
> But God commendeth his love toward us in that, while we were yet sinners, Christ died for us (Rom. 5:6-8).

God saw us "when we were yet without strength" (Rom. 5:6), and sent His Son to live sinlessly and die for us, overcoming our natural inability. He looked on us "while we were yet sinners" (Rom. 5:8), and gave His Son to die that our guilt might be removed. Moreover, God's love was extended to us "when we were enemies" (Rom. 5:10), to subdue our hostility and make it possible for us to live at peace with Him. Occasionally a person has been willing to die for an upright man. Someone might dare to die for the good man in order to make an impact for righteousness. This is quite possible. That God should display His love for a sinful and rebellious mankind, however, is incredible to the human mind, but in it the believer finds a solid basis for his faith.

C. *Guaranteed by Union With the Living Christ*

The Christian's hope of glory is also verified by the present activity of the living Christ. Paul said,

> Much more then, being now justified by his blood, we shall be saved from wrath through him.
> For if, when we were enemies, we were reconciled to God by the death of his Son, much more, being reconciled, we shall be saved by his life (Rom. 5:9, 10).

God has done the greater thing in providing salvation for men, and therefore believers with certainty may expect Him to do the lesser — to provide final deliverance from sin and death. While living upon earth, Christians are subjected to temptation, sometimes fall, and anticipate physical death. However, the fact that Jesus Christ lives, and that those who trust Him are united with Him in a living union, is absolute assurance of final victory. Jesus Christ is not dead. He lives, and believers share His resurrection life. I Corinthians 6:17 declares, "But he that is joined unto the Lord is one spirit." Therefore, believers know the truth that Paul expressed, "When Christ, who is our life, shall appear, then shall ye also appear with him in glory" (Col. 3:4).

The knowledge that Jesus Christ lives should set you to singing! It should give you a heart overflowing with gratitude and praise, enabling you to exult in God.

> And not only so, but we also joy in God through our Lord Jesus Christ, by whom we have now received the reconciliation (Rom. 5:11).

"To joy in God" is the climax of Christian privilege. What a contrast from the picture of the first three chapters of Romans! They presented God, the divine Judge of the universe, in His majesty and holiness. Before Him every person heard the verdict "guilty." Every mouth was stopped and every man realized that his works could not earn him right standing with the Lord. Beginning in Romans 3:21, the glorious truth of salvation is presented. Jesus Christ, God's eternal Son, died for sinners. In so doing He made provision for man's weakness, paid for sin's guilt, and removed the barrier between Himself and man. Therefore, the believer can rejoice in God, who, to him is no longer a condemning Judge, but a forgiving Heavenly Father.

Friend, do you suffer from deep feelings of guilt? Are you burdened with worry and fear? Are you plagued by a sense of loneliness and insignificance? Christ alone can meet your need. Believe God's Word and accept the Lord Jesus as your Savior. You will receive forgiveness and freedom from guilt. You will also find strength to live a new life, and you will no longer be lonely and afraid. You will know that you are a child of God, the object of His love, and that you are destined for a glorious eternity. You will never need to feel lonely or worthless again. You will have the assurance that God loves you and cares for you, and that you have a rich and rewarding future.

7

From Ruin to Redemption

Every person is both an individual being and a member of the human race. As an individual he is not exactly like any other person on earth, and needs a certain amount of freedom to express himself and make his own unique contribution to his fellow men. However, he also lives in close relationship with others. Because each person exists in his own separate body, has his own thoughts, and makes some decisions entirely on his own, does not mean he should forget that he is also part of a family, a community, a country, and the world of mankind. John Donne was right when he wrote, "No man is an island, entire of itself; every man is a piece of the continent, a part of the main; if a clod be washed away by the sea, Europe is the less, as well as if a promontory were, as well as if a manor of thy friends or of thine own were; any man's death diminishes me, because I am involved in mankind; and therefore never send to know for whom the bell tolls; it tolls for thee."

The Bible recognizes both the autonomy of the individual and the solidarity of the human race. The prophet Ezekiel expressed the importance of personal responsibility when he denounced the use of a proverb in Israel which said, "The fathers have eaten sour grapes, and the children's teeth are set on edge" (Ezek. 18:2). Those who uttered this saying were accusing God of injustice. They felt that their national difficulties were a judgment upon the sins of their forefathers, and that they themselves did not deserve such treatment. Ezekiel told them not to make this accusation, for the Lord had declared to him,

> Behold, all souls are mine . . . the soul that sinneth, it shall die (Ezek. 18:4).

This verse expresses a concept implicit to the entire Bible; namely, that each person is responsible to God for his own conduct.

However, the Scriptures also recognize the solidarity of the human family. The sins of the parents often have an effect upon succeeding generations. When God prohibited idol worship, He warned that He would pass judgment,

> . . . visiting the iniquity of the fathers upon the children unto the third and fourth generation of them that hate me (Exod. 20:5).

This passage of Scripture does not teach that God holds children responsible for the evil deeds of their parents, but that because of parental sins some children are victims of social diseases, live in grinding poverty, or grow up without proper moral guidance. Every person comes into a world filled with problems not of his own making, problems he must face and seek to solve.

The solidarity of the human race is also the basis for the recognized principle of representation. Americans, for example, are implicated and involved in all the consequences of the action taken by their representatives in Congress. These men act for the individual citizens they represent. These three things, individual responsibility, human solidarity, and the representative principle, are factors of life which must be understood for a proper approach to Romans 5:12-21. In these verses the apostle Paul discusses two representative men — Adam and Christ. The first man fell, and his evil deed brought sin and death to the whole human race. On the other hand, the second Man, Jesus Christ, lived a perfect life and died a death He did not deserve, bringing salvation and life to all who become united with Him through faith.

I. THE FIRST ADAM — RUINATION AND DEATH

The presence of human wickedness and the reality of physical death are undeniable. Apart from the Bible, however, no logical explanation of their origin or purpose can be given.

A. *The Origin of Sin and Death*

The three opening chapters of the Bible declare that the first man disobeyed God, and this is how human sin and death entered the world. Paul, in Romans 5, viewed the story of Adam and his fall as the explanation for the universality of sin and death.

> Wherefore, as by one man sin entered into the world, and death by sin, and so death passed upon all men, for all have sinned.

> . . . even so by the righteousness of one the free gift came upon all men unto justification of life (Rom. 5:12, 18).

(The words from verse 18 are included here because the thought begun in verse 12 is not completed until verse 18.) He declares that all men are wicked and subject to death because of Adam's sin. The idea is not merely that every person in imitation of Adam commits sin, but that all men are guilty and depraved by virtue of their *relationship* to him. Paul uses the aorist tense in the words "for all have sinned," meaning "for all sinned in Adam."

Theologians have given various explanations of how all men sinned in Adam. Some emphasize the fact of racial solidarity, declaring that all mankind is genetically related to Adam, while others maintain the representative principle, feeling that Adam acted as federal head of the race. It is not important to detail the means by which Adam's sin is passed on to humanity. Paul simply makes the assertion that all men sinned in Adam, and does not discuss how.

B. *The Reigning Power of Death*

The apostle speaks of death as ruling like a powerful tyrant. In verse 14 he declares that "death reigned from Adam to Moses." In the Bible this term never means extinction of being. The basic thought is that of separation. Therefore, when Paul says that because of Adam's sin death passed upon all men, he is not speaking merely of the fact that someday every person's heart stops beating. The death which follows sin is first of all spiritual — the invisible alienation from God because of sin. Jesus spoke of spiritual death when He declared that the person who trusts Him "shall not come into judgment, but is *passed from death unto life*" (John 5:24). So did Paul when he wrote, "And you hath he made alive, who were *dead* in trespasses and sins" (Eph. 2:1). Then the Bible also mentions physical death, the parting of the soul from the body, which is actually the outward sign of the invisible fact that man is alienated from God. Finally, the Scriptures speak of eternal death, the state of everlasting separation from God which is the essence of Hell.

Therefore, death has always been an inescapable reality for every person. This fact is established in Romans 5 where we read that those who lived before the giving of the Mosaic law were estranged from God and died, even though they had not disobeyed a direct command as Adam had.

> For until the law sin was in the world; but sin is not imputed when there is no law.
>
> Nevertheless, death reigned from Adam to Moses, even over them that had not sinned after the similitude of Adam's transgression . . . (Rom. 5:13, 14).

Though these descendants of Adam were not guilty of transgression by violating an expressed command of God, they were nevertheless guilty of sin. Paul said, "Sin was in the world." Men acted against the light of creation (Rom. 1:20, 21) and conscience (Rom. 2:14, 15), but since they had no objective law, they were not held accountable to God as transgressors. By their sinful tendencies and deeds, however, they revealed that they were separated from God through Adam's fall. Moreover, the fact that they all died physically indicates that the sentence of death had indeed passed upon all men. To summarize, these people were not guilty of transgressing God's expressed commands, but they still had inherited both guilt and defilement from Adam. Death, spiritual and physical, reigned like a tyrant over them.

C. *The Despotic Rule of Sin*

Sin is also presented as exercising cruel power over men. Death and sin are vitally related to one another. The people who lived prior to the written law, and those who have never been in touch with His special revelation in Christ, are under the power of death through their sin, but their guilt is mitigated because they have only the light of nature and conscience. However, those who have received special revelation are guilty of transgression when they fail to obey God. Therefore, the apostle refers to the law, declaring that when men received its specific commands and prohibitions, their sin and guilt increased. Paul says,

> Moreover, the law entered, that the offense might abound. But where sin abounded, grace did much more abound;
>
> That as sin hath reigned unto death, even so might grace reign through righteousness unto eternal life by Jesus Christ, our Lord (Rom. 5:20, 21).

The law of Moses came in, appearing alongside sin which was already present. The law therefore caused neither man's guilt nor his sinfulness, but showed him exactly what sin is, increasing his responsibility. In addition, the law actually had the effect of making men more sinful. The presence of a specific law often stimulates sin by arousing a spirit of rebellion. The law simply revealed more fully the principle of sin which was already present in the world, preparing men for the good news of deliverance from its power and penalty.

The apostle Paul therefore traces all human sin and death to the first Adam. Because of *his* disobedience every person has come into the world both depraved and guilty. Death ruled as king even over those who had not received special revelation from God, and thus were not guilty of deliberately violating a specific commandment. Furthermore, the sin of Adam — not the law — is the ultimate source of depravity and guilt, even for those who have received specific prohibitions and commands from God.

II. THE LAST ADAM — REDEMPTION

Christ is the representative Man who brings deliverance from sin and death. In I Corinthians 15:45 Paul refers to Jesus Christ as the "last Adam," and in verse 47 of this same chapter he points to the Lord Jesus as the "second man." Adam, therefore, the first man, is a counterpart of Jesus Christ.

> . . . [Adam] who is the figure [*tupos*] of him that was to come (Rom. 5:14).

A. *The Provision of Salvation and Life*

Jesus Christ, the last Adam, brought righteousness and life to men who were slaves of sin and death. Paul thus contrasts the grace of God which comes through the Lord Jesus with the transgression of the first Adam.

> But not as the offense, so also is the free gift. For if through the offense of one [the] many are dead, much more the grace of God, and the gift by grace, which is by one man, Jesus Christ, hath abounded unto [the] many (Rom. 5:15).

The Lord Jesus is the progenitor of a new race of redeemed men, and the blessings which His people derive through Him are far greater than the curse which Adam transmitted to his descendants.

The glorious truth that Jesus Christ is the representative of a new humanity of redeemed people is summed up in verses 18 and 19, where the apostle clearly states the antithesis between Adam and Christ.

> Therefore, as by the offense of one judgment came upon all men to condemnation, even so by the righteousness of one the free gift came upon all men unto justification of life.

> For as by one man's disobedience many were made sinners,
> so by the obedience of one shall many be made righteous
> (Rom. 5:18, 19).

Paul here used the language of the law court, speaking of condemnation and acquittal. The verb *kathistemi,* rendered "were made" in the King James Version, is a legal term and should be translated "appointed," or "declared." In other words, God as Judge declared men to be sinners because of their relationship to Adam and his *one* offense. Speaking of Christ, the apostle Paul refers to His *one* act of righteousness. The term "righteousness of one" literally means "one man's act of righteousness." This "act of righteousness" is the death of Jesus Christ, when, after living in perfect obedience to God as man's substitute, he paid the price for human sin.

As sin and death entered the world through Adam, so salvation and life through Jesus Christ have been provided. The disobedience of Adam, even apart from the sins men commit, brought death to the race. Thus, the righteousness of Christ, apart from the good works which a child of God performs after his salvation, brings eternal life.

B. *The Reign of Grace unto Eternal Life*

Mankind without Jesus Christ lives under the power of sin and death. However, their tyranny is ended for those who are united to Jesus Christ. Believers, having entered the realm of grace, have a righteous standing before God, and are also the possessors of eternal life.

> That as sin hath reigned unto death, even so might grace
> reign through righteousness unto eternal life by Jesus Christ,
> our Lord (Rom. 5:21).

The truth that sin and salvation are bound together in Adam and Christ is perfectly understandable when we recognize the obvious fact that men are a corporate unity. We do not live alone. Each is affected by what others do. The careless driver endangers the lives of many, and may bring about the death of someone who always drives carefully. Whether we like it or not, the solidarity of the human race cannot be denied. Moreover, the representative principle is not unfair. God has been just, because He gave us two representative men. We have the opportunity of choice. Each person who hears the Gospel must make a decision as an autonomous and rational being. He must choose either to remain in the camp of the first Adam, or to receive Jesus Christ and be brought into the new human family — the redeemed.

Having heard the truth, you are personally responsible for what you do with Jesus Christ.

> . . . they who receive abundance of grace and of the gift of righteousness shall reign in life by one, Jesus Christ (Rom. 5: 17).

In other words, you are obliged to make a response toward the action of God. He has provided grace through Jesus Christ. The gift He offers to you is His righteousness — a place of favor in His presence. If you ignore salvation in Christ, you will continue in sin as a member of Adam's fallen race. Accept the Savior, and you will receive peace with God, a new standing, a new experience of joy, and eternal life.

8

From Death to Resurrection

On the basis of your own personal experience, or your observation of those who proclaim they are believers in Jesus Christ, how would you describe a Christian? I am going to present Paul's portrayal of what God considers to be a typical believer, and see if it coincides with your thinking. A Christian is one who, burdened with the consciousness of his guilt before God, has received the Lord Jesus as Savior by an act of faith. He has found peace with God, feels secure in the knowledge that he has been brought into a vital union with the living Christ, and possesses radiant hope for the future. He realizes that he stands in a place of favor and acceptance before God, and has discovered that divine grace is adequate to give him victory over life's trials. He is able to manifest joy in the midst of the pressures of life, and tells those with whom he comes in contact that these trials are making him a better and purer person. When misunderstood or maligned, he becomes neither depressed nor resentful. Furthermore, he lives a life marked by honesty, kindness, and purity.

I am sure most of us agree that the description just given is not an accurate picture of the average Christian today. This is because we are living far below the level God expects of us. But God has made provision for every Christian to enjoy a life marked by peace, victory, and hope; and the sixth chapter of Romans introduces the formula by which this may be achieved. The Bible makes it clear that salvation cannot be earned, but that a life of good works is nevertheless important. Unless a Christian consistently overcomes his evil tendencies and inclinations, he cannot experience the degree of joy that should be his. Though *possessing* peace with God, and *standing* in the place of acceptance with Him, many Christians are not *experiencing* these truths as a dynamic in their lives. Kindness, purity, truthfulness, honesty, and cheerfulness should mark the life of every believer. In this message we will carefully analyze the logic of Paul, who first answers an objection to his teaching of salvation by grace, and then delivers a practical exhortation for Christian living.

I. AN OBJECTION AND ITS ANSWER

Having stated that salvation is by grace through faith alone, Paul anticipated an objection to this doctrine. He knew that many would look upon it as both illogical and immoral.

A. *The Objection Expressed*

Opponents of the doctrine of free grace have always insisted that, since God's grace is displayed most magnificently when He forgives the gravest of sins, every person should become extremely wicked to give God greater opportunity to manifest His grace.

> What shall we say then? Shall we continue in sin, that grace may abound? (Rom. 6:1).

Unfortunately, this protest to the Pauline doctrine of salvation by faith alone has been given apparent credence through the lives of some professing Christians. F. F. Bruce, in his commentary on Romans 6, points out that the Russian monk Rasputin, the evil genius of the Romanov family in its last years of power, actually practiced this idea. He lived in gross sin, contending that each time he repented he experienced the mercy of God in greater measure than if he had not sinned. He continued to pervert the doctrine of grace until the day of his death. Of course, not many today would openly sin, declaring that they were magnifying God's grace. However, many who profess to be Christians are guilty of viewing their sin lightly, and speak glibly of God's gracious forgiveness without really having experienced it. In such cases the person has given only verbal assent to Biblical truths, and has never genuinely received Jesus Christ.

B. *The Answer Stated*

The apostle recoils from the thought that believers should keep on sinning to give God's grace greater opportunity to manifest itself.

> God forbid. How shall we, that are dead to sin, live any longer in it? (Rom. 6:2).

The expression "God forbid" can be accurately stated as, "By no means!" In the strongest of terms, Paul declares that it is utterly unthinkable that people who have died to sin should be dominated by its power.

The apostle's statement does not have reference to the experience of gradually overcoming various sins. Instead, it points to the death of Jesus Christ, and says that the believer died with Him. Before conversion, every person is a fallen son of Adam, and lives in spiritual death and bondage to sin. However, through faith he has entered into a vital union with Jesus Christ, who, after living a perfect life, died for sinners and arose from the grave. Thus, the believer, united with the living Christ who overcame sin, is judged by God to be finished with his old relationship to the first Adam. He now belongs to a new group, and is a member of the newly created humanity destined for a glorious eternity far above the reach of sin and death. Paul is not saying that a true believer will never have evil thoughts or commit acts of sin. However, he does declare that a Christian cannot live under its domination, or be totally subject to its rule, for he is now identified with Jesus Christ.

II. A PICTURE AND ITS SIGNIFICANCE

Paul reinforces his argument that a true believer is dead to sin, suggesting that his readers recall their baptism. Remember that this ordinance had not yet become a subject of controversy in the Early Church. Baptism marked a dividing line in the life of people who turned to Christ from either Judaism or paganism. It indicated the beginning of a completely new life, the cutting off of all ties with the former religion. There were no unbaptized believers in the Early Church. The apostle therefore directs the attention of his readers to this event, which he knew they would all vividly remember.

> Know ye not that, as many of us as were baptized into (unto) Jesus Christ were baptized into (unto) his death?
> Therefore, we are buried with him by baptism into (unto) death, that as Christ was raised up from the dead by the glory of the Father, even so we also should walk in newness of life (Rom. 6:3, 4).

A. *The Picture*

The early believers knew that baptism had only symbolical significance, and was not the means by which salvation is obtained.

> Know ye not that, as many of us as were baptized into Je-
> sus Christ were baptized into his death? (Rom. 6:3).

The preposition translated "into" frequently means "in relation
to." In I Corinthians 10:2, for example, the Israelites who left
Egypt are said to have been "all baptized unto Moses in the
cloud and in the sea." This does not suggest a mystical incorpora-
tion of the nation into Moses, but simply declares that their old
relationship to Egypt was ended, and that Moses was now their
official leader. In essence, Paul asks his readers, "Don't you
realize that in your baptism you signified your death with Christ,
and the end of your old relationship as a member of a sinful and
guilty race?" The apostle elaborates as he continues,

> Therefore, we are buried with him by baptism into death,
> that as Christ was raised up from the dead by the glory of
> the Father, even so we also should walk in newness of life
> (Rom. 6:4).

The burial that is symbolized when the believer goes under the
water is an announcement that the old order is ended. The
phrase "out of the water" signifies resurrection with Christ who is
our new federal Head, and participation in a new life characterized
by victory over sin.

B. *Its Significance*

In addition to depicting the spiritual reality which has taken
place in the believer's life, Christian baptism has a continuing
message of practical significance for every believer. The meaning of baptism is not exhausted the moment one steps from the
water.

1. An assurance and challenge

By pointing back to the death and resurrection of Jesus Christ,
Christian baptism comforts the believer, assuring him that the
price for sin has actually been paid, and that the power of death
has truly been defeated. The Christian can be absolutely certain
of final victory over sin and death.

> For if we have been planted together in the likeness of his
> death, we shall be also in the likeness of his resurrection
> (Rom. 6:5).

Between these two events — our death with Christ, which was realized when we received Him, and our future resurrection, which will take place because of this same union — we are to walk in newness of life. Some Bible students paraphrase this verse, "If we have shared the reality of His death, of which we have undergone the likeness in baptism, we shall also share the reality of His resurrection, of which our present life of victory over sin is a likeness." This interpretation has a great deal of merit because the Greek word *homoioma,* translated "likeness," means "copy," "facsimile," or "reproduction."

The resurrection of the Lord Jesus Christ is both a token that we shall someday experience a resurrection like His, and an indication that we now live in union with Him. Therefore we are challenged to a life of victory over sin by deriving our strength from the living Christ.

2. A logical deduction

In verses 6 through 10 the apostle states the valid conclusion believers may draw from baptism's picture of their death with Christ. He says,

> Knowing this, that our old man is crucified with him, that the body of sin might be destroyed, that henceforth we should not serve sin.
> For he that is dead is freed from sin (Rom. 6:6, 7).

Pointing back to the crucifixion of Jesus Christ, Paul declares that "our old man is crucified with him." Our lost condition, when we stood condemned as members of the sinful human race, is judged by God to have ended when Christ was crucified. Christian friend, the moment you became a believer in Jesus, God united you with Him, completely breaking your relationship to the past. This is what Paul has in mind in Galatians when he says,

> But God forbid that I should glory, except in the cross of our Lord Jesus Christ, by whom the world is crucified unto me, and I unto the world (Gal. 6:14).

Paul uses the perfect tense to denote that the present state of the believer has been produced by the past event of Romans 6:6. God has done this,

> . . . that the body of sin might be destroyed, that henceforth we should not serve sin (Rom. 6:6).

The "body of sin" does not have reference to the human body. Rather, it points to the past solidarity of sin and death, which, as a tyrant, holds mankind in abject slavery. The word translated "destroyed" is *katargeo,* which means "done away" or "rendered inoperative." Paul declares that a new solidarity of righteousness and life through Christ has broken the despotic power of the old order. Therefore, Paul concludes,

> For he that is dead is freed from sin (Rom. 6:7).

In the natural world a dead man can no longer put himself at the service of sin, nor can he be held legally answerable for his wrongdoings. Even as death breaks all earthly relationships and pays all debts, so the man who has died with Christ is completely free from both the bondage and the guilt of his past state.

Paul closes his discussion of the believer's death as portrayed in baptism with a direct reference to Jesus Christ.

> Knowing that Christ, being raised from the dead, dieth no more; death hath no more dominion over him.
> For in that he died, he died unto sin once; but in that he liveth, he liveth unto God (Rom. 6:9, 10).

The Lord Jesus died once, conquered death, and will never die again. He submitted to death that He might destroy its power. When He said, "Father, into thy hands I commend my spirit," and died, He was not admitting defeat. Instead, His death was a sign of the complete routing of sin in a decisive engagement. Paul says concerning Christ that "he died unto sin." The apostle has been personifying sin as a cruel tyrant gaining mastery over men and leading them to eternal destruction. Therefore, he views the death of Jesus as the end of sin's opportunity to overcome the Son of God. Because throughout His life the Lord had successfully resisted every temptation, He could on the cross offer up in death a perfect life. Now, with sin and death defeated, Christ lives unto the Father with these experiences behind Him. Paul applies this glorious truth to believers in the next section.

III. An Exhortation and Its Dynamic

Our oneness with Jesus Christ, as expressed in baptism, is more than a mystical concept in which a Christian is to take great pleasure. True, a believer should never forget that Jesus Christ defeated sin by His perfect life, and conquered death through His resurrection. Nor should he lose sight of the glorious truth that he is now "in Christ," and therefore forever released from his former bondage to sin and its consequences. However, these truths must be made real in the believer's daily experience, for he lives in a world where sin and death are still realities with which he must deal. Therefore Paul declares,

> Likewise, reckon ye also yourselves to be dead indeed unto sin, but alive unto God through Jesus Christ, our Lord (Rom. 6:11).

We are commanded to live as though we had already entered the resurrection life. This imperative is in the present tense, indicating that day by day we must look upon ourselves as dead to sin and alive to God. Many Christians, after struggling vainly to overcome evil in their lives, have found victory upon learning this truth. If a certain sin has you in its grasp, you too can conquer it by applying the truth of Romans 6:11. Whenever the temptation comes, remind yourself that you died to this sin, and that you live in union with the Son of God. This reckoning is not a mere psychological exercise. It possesses a dynamic power, for the Holy Spirit makes effective *in* us that which Christ did *for* us.

If you are a Christian, you need no longer live in bondage to sin. The moment you trusted Jesus Christ you became a member of the new humanity. Your old existence in Adam ceased, and God transferred you to the domain of His beloved Son. In Christ you were "justified from sin," set free completely from its grasp and guilt. All of this can be made real in present experience when by faith you consider yourself "dead indeed unto sin, but alive unto God." By doing this you embrace consciously the full provision of Calvary, both for the remission of your sin and deliverance from its power. Begin today to "keep on reckoning yourself dead to sin and alive to God." This is the means by which you can live the normal Christian life of peace, holiness, and joyous hope.

9

From Sin's Tyranny to God's Dominion

One day the Lord Jesus aroused the indignation of His self-righteous audience by declaring that every person on earth is a slave of sin. He said,

> . . . Whosoever committeth sin is the servant of sin (John 8: 34).

Most people are inclined to disagree with this statement. They gladly acknowledge that the drunkard is ruled by alcohol, that the libertine is in bondage to lust, and that the sexual pervert or kleptomaniac is unable to control his natural tendencies. However, they react unfavorably when told that they themselves are the servants of sin. In the first place, they do not agree that any act is inherently sinful, because they do not believe in a personal God and the moral law. Furthermore, they rather indignantly assert that whenever they do things Christians call sinful, it is because they choose to, and not because they are enslaved.

Whether they admit it or not, however, all are victims of certain habits, self-indulgences and pleasures. Not every person engages in extreme practices like those of the gunman, harlot, or sex fiend, but everyone has his own selfish desires and inclinations. The words of Jesus Christ stand true: everyone who sins is a slave. Sin, you see, is not to be looked upon as a series of individual offenses, having no relation to the past or future. Man's sinful nature is such that he must be considered spiritually sick. Just as a person who is ill is in the grip of his disease, and will finally die if the malady is not arrested, so the sinner is a slave of sin. God must intervene and break its power, or the sinner, under the sentence of eternal death, is doomed.

When a person is saved, however, he is delivered from sin's guilt and power. Therefore a Christian, when he is baptized, portrays that he died to his old standing as a guilty and defiled sinner. Through faith in Christ he has become a member of the new, redeemed humanity, and in his daily life he is to demonstrate the reality of his new position before God.

> Likewise, reckon ye also yourselves to be dead indeed unto sin, but alive unto God through Jesus Christ, our Lord (Rom. 6:11).

The present tense of the command given in this verse indicates that we daily and constantly are to consider ourselves dead to sin and alive to God. We who know Christ need not live in bondage to sin. If we will but believe what God has said about the end of our old standing as guilty and depraved members of a fallen race, and apply this to our daily lives, we are assured of achieving victory over sin.

The last half of Romans 6 teaches that the believer is placed into a new servitude, the dominion of God. To set forth this truth, Paul personifies sin and righteousness, depicting them as masters between whom men must make a choice. To serve sin is to be under the domination of Satan, remaining in spiritual death as a member of the fallen race. To serve righteousness is to be a servant of God, a member of the new humanity which possesses eternal life.

I. DELIVERANCE INTO GOD'S DOMINION

Since believers have been delivered from the kingdom of darkness into the realm of light, Paul solemnly forbids them to permit sin to be sovereign in their lives.

> Let not sin, therefore, reign in your mortal body, that ye should obey it in its lusts (Rom. 6:12).

The believer's body is mortal, because it has not yet been delivered from physical death. Christians are waiting for the redemption of the body at the Lord's coming. Furthermore, Christians can be tempted to sin through bodily desires. This is not because the body in itself is sinful, but because sin is ready to assume control through it. Man's evil tendencies are not eradicated when he becomes a Christian. Satan will use man's normal physical desires to lead him to sin. However, God does not intend that those who have been united with Christ should be controlled by sin.

> For sin shall not have dominion over you; for ye are not under the law but under grace (Rom. 6:14).

To live under law is to seek forgiveness and eternal life through self-efforts, which no one can possibly attain. Even the Mosaic law was unable to help men earn salvation, for no one was able to keep its commandment perfectly. The godly Israelite was delivered from sin's guilt and power when, recognizing his total inability to please God by his own works, he presented an animal sacrifice. This was his admission that he needed forgiveness on the basis of God's grace alone. Paul's statement, "Ye are not under law," is primarily an announcement that Christians do not live under a legal system of righteousness by works. Instead, they have been transferred from the rule of law to the realm of grace through faith in Christ. Therefore, though all individual efforts to escape sin's bondage are doomed to failure, believers are assured that they can successfully overcome it because of their union with the living Christ. They have been delivered from the dominion of sin and death into the kingdom of righteousness and life.

II. The Experience of God's Dominion

A true believer will have an earnest desire to be delivered from sin's power. He will hate sin, for he knows that it is the monstrous evil which made necessary the Lord's suffering and death on Calvary. The child of God realizes that Christ came to destroy sin, and therefore does not coldly calculate that a life of wickedness will magnify God's grace. It is psychologically impossible for a person to trust Christ and desire a life of sin. Paul has clearly demonstrated this in the first half of Romans 6.

In verse 15 he considers a new question. What about a believer deliberately committing an act of sin from time to time?

> What then? Shall we sin, because we are not under the law, but under grace? . . . (Rom. 6:15).

A person might reason that since God freely forgives sin, and provides salvation apart from works, an occasional act of sin might be considered to be of small consequence.

A. *Recognition of Only One Master*

Paul expresses his abhorrence of such a thought in the ensuing verses. Personifying sin and righteousness as rulers over slaves, he points out that no man can serve two masters. Christians are no longer the slaves of sin, but of righteousness; therefore, it is God whom they must serve.

> Know ye not that to whom ye yield yourselves servants to obey, his servants ye are whom ye obey, whether of sin unto death, or of obedience unto righteousness?
>
> But God be thanked, that whereas ye were the servants of sin, ye have obeyed from the heart that form of doctrine which was delivered you.
>
> Being, then, made free from sin, ye became the servants of righteousness (Rom. 6:16-18).

Paul does not deny that Christians may sometimes have evil thoughts or conduct themselves in a sinful manner. Nor does he imply that an act of sin causes a believer to lose his justification. He is simply asserting that no believer should think in terms of serving two masters. He is not to mentally make provision for even occasional acts of sin. Instead, he must consciously recognize that wickedness no longer has any claim upon him, and that he now belongs to a new Master — God.

B. *Presentation of Self to God*

Paul further reveals how a believer is to experience the reality of God's dominion. He declares that he is using the analogy of the slave market "because of the infirmity of your flesh." Christians, though justified and in Christ, are still subject to evil thoughts and inclinations. This truth was stated by the apostle in verse 12, which speaks of the mortal body and its lusts. The Christian therefore must not depend upon himself, thinking he can achieve mastery over sin in his own strength. He is to recognize that he is so constituted that he must be a slave, either to the forces of evil or to God. Therefore Paul declares,

> I speak after the manner of men because of the infirmity of your flesh; for as ye have yielded your members servants to uncleanness and to iniquity, unto iniquity; even so now yield your members servants to righteousness, unto holiness (Rom. 6:19).

The secret of holy living is found in the yielding of self to God. The verb translated "yield" is in the aorist tense, meaning "to present in a decisive act of dedication." The Roman believers had formerly allowed themselves to become slaves to uncleanness and to one sinful deed after another — to greater and greater wickedness. Now, however, they should submit themselves to God, once for all, giving to Him all their faculties and powers. The command that was issued in verse 13 is repeated in verse 19, "Stop handing over your members as weapons of unrighteousness to sin, but hand over yourselves once for all to God . . . and your members as weapons of righteousness."

This decision to submit to God as Master and Sovereign is made at the time of salvation. However, the full implications will be gradually realized. Therefore sanctification, victory over sin in our daily lives, is a process of growth. This is indicated in the last half of verse 19, which sets forth our progressive submission to God's will in contrast to the ever-deepening control of sin prior to salvation. Before we were saved, we presented "our members as servants to uncleanness and to iniquity," each sin conditioning us to yield more easily to the next. In sanctification the process is reversed. Having presented ourselves to God, we experience day-by day growth as we make decisions regarding the moral issues that confront us. Every time we yield to what we know is the will of God, we are conditioned to respond more easily the next time, and we gradually grow in likeness to Jesus Christ. This is practical holiness through the process of progressive sanctification.

III. THE RESULT OF GOD'S DOMINION

The believer who thus consciously recognizes God as his Master and yields to Him finds true spiritual freedom. Instead of a life marked by anxiety, frustration and abject slavery to sin, he enjoys a sense of fulfillment, fellowship with God, and victory over sin. He also becomes increasingly conscious of God's presence and direction. Therefore Paul concludes,

> But now being made free from sin, and become servants to God, ye have your fruit unto holiness, and the end everlasting life (Rom. 6:22).

The two key words, both well-known Biblical terms, are "holiness" and "everlasting life."

A. *Holiness*

The fruit of a life of voluntary subjection to God is "holiness." The Greek word used here is sometimes rendered "sanctification." This term and its cognates, as well as the Hebrew words which are rendered "holiness" and "sanctification" in the Old Testament, are used in reference to God, to things, and to people.

1. The Old Testament Concept

Applied to God they signify His separation from and transcendency over all His creation, or emphasize the absolute purity of His nature. Applied to objects, like the tabernacle and its furnishings, these words designated withdrawal from common employment and being set aside for God's service. In relation to people these terms in the Old Testament usually had reference to ceremonial cleanness through the divinely established ritual of the law, and occasionally to ethical righteousness.

2. The New Testament Meaning

In the New Testament, when used of people, holiness is presented in two aspects, which must be distinguished. *Positional* holiness is the perfect standing believers have in Christ. They are set apart for God and are no longer subject to condemnation. This is *imputed* holiness. *Experimental* holiness depicts the moral quality imparted to believers because of union with Christ, their new birth, and their possession of the indwelling Holy Spirit. Whenever these words speak of man's *imparted* holiness they describe only relative goodness as contrasted to the absolute purity of God. As previously noted in this study, believers are still subject to temptation, and in this life will never achieve perfect holiness. However, the Christian's character and walk will be marked by righteousness, and, as an obedient believer, he will grow more and more into the likeness of the Savior. This imparted holiness is the subject of Romans 6:22.

B. *Eternal Life*

The believers can also look forward to eternal life. The verse concludes, ". . . and the end everlasting life." This term, "everlasting (or eternal) life," always means more than mere endless existence. The Bible sometimes speaks of it as the present possession of the believer, as when Jesus said,

> Verily, verily, I say unto you, He that heareth my word, and believeth on him that sent me, hath everlasting life, and shall not come into judgment, but is passed from death unto life (John 5:24).

Eternal life, then, is a gift imparted by God to those who receive Jesus Christ. This takes place when a person is born again, and for this reason regeneration is described as being "born of God" (John 1:13), or "born again" (John 3:3).

Eternal life also denotes the glorious future of believers in Heaven. This is its meaning in Romans 6:23. Paul looks forward to the time when believers will be free from all imperfections, infirmity and temptation. Fellowship with God will be perfect in Heaven, and fullness of joy will be the experience of every child of God. This is the ultimate destiny for all who trust Jesus Christ.

The last verse of Romans 6 set forth in summary the contrast between serving sin or submitting to God.

> For the wages of sin is death, but the gift of God is eternal life through Jesus Christ, our Lord (Rom. 6:23).

Sin pays wages to those who work for it. Its payment is death. Whoever lives as a servant of sin is under the reign of law, and therefore sin renders this wage as a matter of debt or obligation. Those who serve sin will receive the exact recompense God's justice requires. However, willing servitude to God places one under the reign of grace. Therefore, instead of wages, God gives a gift; namely, eternal life. The word translated "gift" is *charisma,* which means "grace gift." Salvation is unmerited favor bestowed by God upon those who believe in Jesus Christ. All of salvation has its origin in the love of God.

> For God so loved the world, that he gave his only begotten Son, that whosoever believeth in him should not perish, but have everlasting life (John 3:16).

He is ready to freely bestow salvation upon you, if you will receive Jesus Christ as your Savior.

10

Freedom From Law

The writer of a syndicated newspaper column recently bemoaned man's selfishness and cruelty, declaring that unless individual people can be cured of their greed and inhumanity, the world will never be without wars, riots, racism, and social injustice. The columnist gloomily acknowledged that he did not expect the moral ills of mankind to be remedied. This picture of man's sinfulness strikingly resembles the portrait presented in the first three chapters of Romans. The apostle Paul, however, did not despair like this contemporary writer, because he knew God's remedy for human sin — the substitutionary death, burial, and resurrection of Jesus Christ. By His spotless life Christ defeated the power of sin, by His sacrifice on the cross bore its penalty, and by His resurrection overcame death itself. The Lord Jesus did all of these things *here,* on this planet, and now God bestows forgiveness and eternal life on all who receive Jesus Christ as their personal Savior. These believers are *now* accounted righteous in the sight of their Maker, and are removed from the place of guilt into a position of favor with Him.

After showing that God has provided salvation from human sin the apostle Paul indicated that believers, being the recipients of a new life, are to consider themselves dead to the old way of habitual and ever-increasing sinfulness. Now he takes up a new problem, that of the believer's relationship to the law of Moses, which was still revered by the Jews who had turned to Christ. Even the pagans who had become Christians recognized that the work of Jesus Christ was closely related to the Hebrew faith and the Mosaic law. For this reason, throughout the entire history of the Church, many sincere believers have thought that the Christian life consists of trying to keep the Ten Commandments. However, the epistles of Paul emphatically teach that all attempts to retain salvation through legalistic self-effort are unnecessary and wrong. This is exactly the theme of Romans 7 where the apostle clearly sets forth two related truths: (1) believers have been freed from the principle of the law as a way of life; and (2) the law is totally inadequate to provide victory over sin. God has a better way to lead Christians into a holy life. Even as He came into this world in the person of Jesus Christ to defeat sin, pay its price, and conquer death, so now He is here in the person of the Holy Spirit to empower Christians for godly living.

I. THE LIMITATIONS OF LAW

Human laws operate within certain boundaries. We all know, for example, that the laws of the United States government are not in effect in England. Similarly, when a person dies, the law no longer has any claim upon him — death terminates his obligation to it, as Romans 7:1 says:

> Know ye not, brethren (for I speak to them that know the law), how that the law hath dominion over a man as long as he liveth?

The same is true in the spiritual realm. Death ends the believer's relationship to the law, both for salvation and for holy living. The analogy of marriage is used in Romans 7 to set forth this truth. Under Jewish or Roman law, a woman was bound to her husband as long as he lived. The man could initiate divorce proceedings, but not the wife. Therefore, if she left her husband during his lifetime for another man, she was branded as an adulteress. If he died, however, she was free to marry someone else without incurring disrepute.

> For the woman who hath an husband is bound by the law to her husband as long as he liveth; but if the husband be dead, she is loosed from the law of her husband.
> So, then if, while her husband liveth, she be married to another man, she shall be called an adulteress; but if her husband be dead, she is free from that law, so that she is no adulteress, though she be married to another man (Rom. 7: 2, 3).

Even as death breaks the marriage bond, so death — the believer's death with Christ — severs the bond which formerly yoked him to the law. Christ, by His sinless life, overcame the law, and by His death gave that victory to the believer. United with Christ, the believer is exonerated from the condemnation of the law.

Many people are shocked when they hear Christians talk about being free from the law. They look upon such a declaration as giving license to commit sin and transgress God's commandments. They misunderstand, however, and fail to comprehend the meaning and intent of the law God gave through Moses. The person who reads Exodus, Leviticus, and Deuteronomy discovers that the legal system called the Mosaic law was a unit. It included civil regulations as well as the Ten Commandments. Moreover, since no man was able to keep the law perfectly, it also provided the way of forgiveness through sacrifice. The legal demands showed men their wickedness and inability to save themselves by works, while the sacrifices, on the other hand, revealed God's grace as the means of salvation. The whole Mosaic system came to an end when Jesus Christ died on the cross, and God underscored this truth when the veil of the temple was torn in two from the top to the bottom at the moment of our Lord's death (Matt. 27:51). The believer now is pictured as being "married to Christ," and a comparison is made between the progeny of this new union and that of the old marriage to the law.

> Wherefore, my brethren, ye also are become dead to the law by the body of Christ, that ye should be married to another, even to him who is raised from the dead, that we should bring forth fruit unto God (Rom. 7:4).

Christians are to be fruit-bearers, their lives marked by righteousness. This is in sharp contrast to the product of a life that is lived "in the flesh," the self-effort of an unrenewed sinner to earn God's favor. The religionists of the first century were doing precisely this. They had added oral amplifications to the law through the centuries, which resulted in an extremely complicated code of conduct by which men were to attain favor with God. In so doing, they completely missed God's intent. The Lord gave the law to teach them the depths of human sin and depravity, thus driving them to admit their need of divine grace. The result of all effort "in the flesh" is "fruit unto death"; that is, evil works which bring about eternal alienation from God. This is the point of Romans 7:5.

> For when we were in the flesh, the sinful impulses, which were by the law, did work in our members to bring forth fruit unto death.

The truth of the believer's freedom from law and his union with Christ is then summarized:

> But now we are delivered from the law, that being dead
> in which we were held, that we should serve in newness of
> spirit and not in the oldness of the letter (Rom. 7:6).

By virtue of their death with Christ, believers are released from
the guilt they had incurred by their failure to keep the law of
God, and freed from a life of striving to maintain fellowship with
Him by strenuous self-effort. Now, being no longer bound by
the law, they enjoy a new relationship through their union with
Christ, serving God, not in slavish fear, but in the spirit of love
and dedication.

If you are a Christian, you must abandon all thoughts that by
your own efforts at law-keeping you can please God. In your own
strength you will surely fail. However, to deliver you from a
vain and hopeless struggle for holiness, God has united you with
Christ, and given His Holy Spirit to indwell your body.

II. The Inadequacy of Law

Having set forth the truth that believers are not to think in
terms of pleasing God by legalistic self-effort, the apostle now
deals with the problem of the believer's relationship to the Ten
Commandments in particular. The Jewish believers could well
understand that the sacrificial system had been fulfilled in Christ,
but undoubtedly wondered why Paul would declare that believers
had died not only to sin, but also to the law. I hear them say,
"What about the Ten Commandments? Aren't they good? Aren't
believers under obligation to keep them?" In answer to these
queries, Romans 7:7-13 clearly teaches that the Decalogue is indeed good, and it does perform a useful spiritual service. However, it cannot enable a person to live a holy life.

A. *The Function of the Law*

The apostle immediately sets the mind of Jewish believers at
rest by declaring that the law is good.

> What shall we say then? Is the law sin? God forbid . . .
> (Rom. 7:7).

He amplifies this declaration by recalling his own experience. He
had been brought up in the strictest tradition of the Hebrew faith,
first as a boy at home, then as a young student at the feet of
Gamaliel in Jerusalem. He said that his contact with the Ten

Commandments revealed to him the nature, the intensity, the result, the perverting power, and the deceitfulness of sin.

1. The Nature of Sin Revealed

The fact of human sin is apparent to all, but the natural man does not understand its nature. He sees only the outward acts which harm people or deprive them of certain rights, but does not perceive that sin is a condition of the heart. Through the Ten Commandments Paul was awakened to see that sin resides within, and does not consist in mere external words and deeds.

> . . . Nay, I had not known sin, but by the law; for I had not known coveting, except the law had said, Thou shalt not covet (Rom. 7:7).

Undoubtedly for many years Paul was much like the rich young ruler who came to Jesus with the question, "Good Master, what shall I do that I may inherit eternal life?" When Jesus enumerated a few of the commandments the young man replied, "All these have I observed from my youth." The Lord then said, "One thing thou lackest; go thy way, sell whatever thou hast, and give to the poor . . . and follow me." The young man went away sorrowful, for Jesus had put His finger upon the sin in his life, that of covetousness. The illicit desire for things meant more to him than obedience to God. His goodness had been merely external.

Paul had the same superficial concept of goodness until one day he began to reflect upon the tenth commandment. He had considered himself blameless as far as the other commandments were concerned, but now realized that he had been guilty of every kind of improper desire. He saw that his righteousness was only external, and that in reality he was a sinner justly exposed to God's wrath. Whether this realization came to him rather early in life, or after he had witnessed the death of Stephen, we do not know. However, the knowledge that he was a guilty sinner undoubtedly played a part in preparing him for that day he surrendered to Christ on the road to Damascus.

2. The Intensity of Sin Portrayed

In addition to showing him the nature of sin, the tenth commandment, "Thou shalt not covet," also revealed the intensity, the exceeding sinfulness of sin. When Paul realized that his illicit desires were evil, he found forbidden things increasingly appealing. Thus he learned that sin is rebellion, and that when the law reveals and defines sin, it also incites active disobedience.

> But sin, taking occasion by the commandment, wrought in me all manner of coveting. For apart from the law sin is dead (Rom. 7:8).

Without the existence of a law, sin is present but men are hardly aware of it. However, when something is forbidden or placed out of bounds it becomes fascinating. Men naturally desire it, and thus find themselves violating specific laws. Therefore, though the law reveals the fact that sin is rebellion, it cannot overcome this tendency in man.

3. The Result of Sin Unfolded

In addition to revealing the nature and intensity of sin, the law also made known to Saul of Tarsus that the "wages of sin is death." He had fancied himself to be spiritually alive, and thought he was making progress through his own works of righteousness, but, when the true meaning of the Tenth Commandment made its impact upon his heart, sin sprang to life. He began to realize that through his own works he could never attain glory. He now saw himself as a guilty sinner and spiritually dead, needing both divine forgiveness and a supernaturally imparted life.

> For I was alive apart from the law once; but when the commandment came, sin revived, and I died (Rom. 7:9).

4. Perverting Power of Sin Uncovered

The law, when spiritually apprehended, also reveals the power of sin to pervert and twist that which is good. Paul declares that the commandment was "ordained to life." He means that God's holy requirements were given that man might enjoy true life and fellowship with his Maker through obedience to them. However, as previously noted, the prohibitions of God's law arouse the spirit of rebellion in sinful humans, leading them into deeper sin and guilt. The law shows that sin is perverting. For example, sin takes the beauty of love and turns it into lust, and the desire for independence into greed. The natural man deludes himself into thinking that he can find satisfaction in sin, and that he will escape the final consequences of eternal death, but the person who truly understands the law of God knows better.

> And the commandment, which was ordained to life, I found to be unto death.
>
> For sin, taking occasion by the commandment, deceived me, and by it slew me (Rom. 7:10, 11).

Though the law reveals the inward nature of sin, its rebellion, its consequences, and its perverting power, it is nevertheless good and holy, for it is the voice of God. This is what Paul says in Romans 7:12,

> Wherefore, the law is holy, and the commandment holy, and just, and good.

Its goodness is to be found in that it was designed for man's spiritual benefit and eternal welfare, but, because of human inability, it never has secured salvation for anyone. Its function is twofold: (1) to show men their deep inner depravity and utter helplessness to save themselves, and (2) to point them to Jesus Christ. Under Moses, the law included within its scope the teaching of grace through the sacrifices and offerings. Today, however, the law directs men to Calvary.

> Was then that which is good made death unto me? God forbid. But sin, that it might appear sin, working death in me by that which is good — that sin by the commandment might become exceedingly sinful (Rom. 7:13).

Christian friend, are you living a defeated life week after week? Do not seek victory over sin by your own human effort. You may awaken with good resolutions every morning, but every evening you will once again recognize that you have failed God in many ways. You can never live a godly life in your own strength. Even as you once received the Lord Jesus Christ by simple faith, so now you are to live your Christian life in humble dependence upon Him. God, having united you with Jesus Christ, has become part of your life through the indwelling Holy Spirit.

Unsaved friend, your own works will never suffice to earn favor with God. The law can only condemn you. Acknowledge your sin, believe that Jesus Christ died to pay its price, and accept Him as your Lord and Savior. Before you can live a Christian life you need Christ within your heart. Christ is here. Trust Him today.

11

The Struggle With Sin

The human personality is sometimes difficult to understand. A man owning a factory may be heartless and coldly calculating toward his employees, but kind and tender to his grandchildren. A person who is living in gross immorality may be at the same time relatively honest and truthful in his business dealings. For this reason people often speak of "the good that is in the worst of us and the bad that is in the best of us." In addition to possessing this blend of good and evil inclinations, most people experience inner conflicts when facing moral decisions. The apostle Paul vividly described such an inward spiritual struggle in the book of Romans. He declared that he knew what he should do, and felt that he ought to, but somehow just didn't do it. He added that even when he earnestly desired to do what was right, he found himself powerless. Then, analyzing his inward battle, he discovered that the reason for this inability was indwelling sin. Finally he realized that he could achieve victory only by looking outside himself and turning to the Lord. Then, learning that God had entered his life in the person of the Holy Spirit he knew the way to a life of holiness and true joy.

I. THE CONFLICT DESCRIBED

The apostle graphically portrays his spiritual struggle. He does not tell us whether he went through this experience before or after he met Jesus Christ, and Bible students have sharply disagreed with one another on this score. Some have unequivocally declared that he wrestled with this problem while still a young Pharisee. Others assert that it took place shortly after his conversion to Christ, before he saw clearly that he had been delivered from the Old Testament legal system. Still others look upon Paul as desperately trying and miserably failing in his efforts to overcome indwelling sin throughout his entire earthly life. They look upon this as the normal Christian experience. Obviously, not all of these views can be correct, and we should carefully study the description of the conflict before seeking to pinpoint the time of the struggle to which it has reference. The portrait Paul paints of himself in Romans 7:14-25 first depicts him as knowing the right and approving it, but simply failing to perform it. Then, secondly, it shows that though he passionately desired to be kind, honest, and pure, he was unable to reach these goals.

A. *The Right Acknowledged But Not Performed*

Paul's problem was not one of ignorance of God's demands. He knew the Old Testament Scriptures and recognized that they had their origin in God. Therefore he said,

> For we know that the law is spiritual . . . (Rom. 7:14).

This statement teaches that the legal system given through Moses is the result of the working of God's Holy Spirit. The apostle willingly approved of the law, declaring that its demands are right and good. However, he found within his nature something opposed to God and His laws, so that he always failed to do what he knew to be right.

> . . . but I am carnal, sold under sin.
> For that which I do I understand not . . . (Rom. 7:14, 15).

Paul recognized himself to be a fallen creature, a member of the sinful human race, and enslaved to the sin principle. He was baffled by his own conduct. He could not understand himself, because, though he knew what was right and acknowledged that he ought to do it, he nevertheless did not perform it.

The predicament here described has been faced by multitudes of both saved and unsaved people. Ovid the Roman poet said, "I see and approve the better course, but I follow the worse one." This is common human experience. Most people will admit that in actual practice they are not nearly as good as they know they ought to be. Some frankly declare that they have no desire to live the way they know they should. They express admiration for people who live on a high moral and spiritual plane, but feel that such a life for them would be boredom. Others, acknowledging that they should be more honest, kind, and pure than they are, find comfort in saying that no one is perfect, and delight in pointing to others whom they consider to be greater offenders than they. However, if pressed, they will admit that, though they know what they ought to do, they are not doing it.

B. *Goodness Desired But Not Attained*

To approve what is right while acknowledging one's own failure is one thing, but to have an earnest desire for holiness is quite another. This is exactly how Paul described his own experience. He passionately longed for holiness, but somehow wasn't able to live that kind of life. He said in perplexity,

> . . . for what I would, that do I not; but what I hate, that do I (Rom. 7:15).

He further declared that the problem does not reside within the will. Paul wanted to do right, but he didn't know how to perform it. His efforts to do good were met with constant failure, for he fell into the evil thoughts and deeds he had hoped to avoid.

> . . . for to will is present with me, but how to perform that which is good I find not.
> For the good that I would, I do not; but the evil which I would not, that I do (Rom. 7:18, 19).

In fact, Paul actually found pleasure in meditating upon the holy law of God. He said,

> For I delight in the law of God after the inward man (Rom. 7:22).

Here then is the portrait of a man who knows what is right but is puzzled by his wrong conduct; he longs to be pure, hates evil, and actually loves the holy law of God, yet is unable to deliver himself from slavery to sin.

Is Paul here describing himself before he turned to Jesus Christ? Did this struggle occur after he received the Lord Jesus, but before he was instructed regarding his relationship to the law of Moses? The answer is that this passage of Scripture applies both to Paul's experience before he became a Christian and his life after he was saved. It pictures any person trying to be morally upright, seeking to please God in his own strength.

Many unsaved people never go through deep inner conflict when facing moral issues. They are blessed with likable qualities which enable them to conduct themselves in a respectable manner, and are content with outward conformity to accepted norms of conduct. Other non-Christians know what God's moral law requires, through conscience and general revelation, and acknowledge they should obey it. However, they also do not become exercised about the matter of personal holiness. They think that the pleasures of sin are worth whatever risks are involved. A third group long for deliverance from degrading or harmful practices, but are unsuccessful in all their strivings. A fourth class of people realize that true goodness before God consists in more than mere external obedience to certain rules, and long to rid their lives of evil. However, they find themselves frustrated because they are helpless in their battle with sin.

Many psychologists declare that every person has within him not only the ego, the center of his personality, but also the id and super-ego. They claim that conflicts arise because the id, the source of the lower inclinations and passions, and the super-ego, the fountainhead of men's higher longings, both make demands upon the ego. While this is only a theory and cannot be proven, no one can deny that many non-Christians undergo fierce inner struggles as they are confronted with moral decisions. However, the experience described in Romans 7 cannot be applied in total to an unsaved person. Only one who has trusted Jesus Christ and received the new birth can say, "For I delight in the law of God after the inward man" (Rom. 7:22). On the other hand, this portrayal of warfare and constant defeat in the quest for victory over sin must not be viewed as normal Christian experience. Romans 6:14 declares,

> For sin shall not have dominion over you; for ye are not under the law but under grace.

This passage must be carefully analyzed if one is to see exactly how it fits into the lives of genuine believers.

II. THE STRUGGLE ANALYZED

The apostle Paul, perplexed by his inability to do the things he wanted, was actually amazed that he found himself practicing the very things he hated. His problem, remember, was not lack of knowledge, for he knew the right. His difficulty did not reside in his will, for he earnestly longed to do what God wanted. Nor could he place the blame for his enigma at the door of his emotions, for he found pleasure in God's law, and hated sin. He therefore concluded that his true self, his ego, was being acted upon by some inner force that had become part of his humanity. Therefore he said,

> Now, then, it is no more I that do it, but sin that dwelleth in me (Rom. 7:17).

He repeated this statement in verse 20, then went on to exclaim,

> For I delight in the law of God after the inward man;
> But I see another law in my members, warring against the law of my mind, and bringing me into captivity to the law of sin which is in my members (Rom. 7:22, 23).

The apostle declared that though he knew the right and desired it, and though he now possessed an "inward man" finding joy in God's holy law, he was still unable to achieve spiritual victory because of indwelling sin. He retained the sinful nature he had inherited from Adam, and it infected or tainted everything he said and did. This sin nature was neither removed nor changed when he became a Christian. Therefore, though Paul experienced the new birth, and though this "inward man" loved God and longed to do His will, indwelling sin continued to hinder his achieving the holy life he desired so much.

No Christian truly understands himself unless he clearly recognizes that he still possesses the old sin nature, even though he has received new life from God. This evil nature has neither died nor been removed. True, in Romans 6:6 Paul declares that "our old man is crucified," but he is not speaking of the sin nature which we inherit from Adam. He is saying that the believer's position as guilty and depraved is now ended. God no longer looks upon the sinner as he is "in Adam," but as he is "in Christ." Therefore, this statement of Romans 6 must not be interpreted as declaring that the evil nature is eradicated. The new nature imparted by God in regeneration delights in His will and desire to do it. However, the old Adamic nature is still present, and when the lofty thoughts and aspirations of the new life come in touch with it they are polluted, even as the pure waters of a spring are contaminated after they leave their source.

The reason you are unable to be the kind of person you wish to be is because of indwelling sin. As long as you strive in your own strength to overcome your evil tendencies you will experience defeat and frustration. Romans 7 depicts such a person by his own effort seeking to conquer evil. Even the Christian is powerless to do it, for he still possesses the old sinful nature he inherited from Adam. Paul speaks of this when he refers to the "law of the mind" and the "inward man" which come into constant conflict with the "law of sin" indwelling every person.

III. THE BATTLE RESOLVED

Some believers therefore conclude that since no man is able in his own strength to overcome sin, it is normal for a Christian to have one defeat after another in his spiritual struggle. This is, however, contrary to the strong assertion Paul made in Romans 6,

> For sin shall not have dominion over you; for ye are not under the law but under grace (Rom. 6:14).

True, a warfare is being waged between two spiritual kingdoms — the "law of God" and the "law of sin" — on the battlefield of the human personality. This is an intense conflict, and many Christians expect that, although they will win the final war, they will lose every battle along the way. This is because they have been carrying out the skirmishes in the wrong way. They have been fighting in their own strength, and whenever a person does this he is overcome by the awesome power of indwelling sin. Realizing that this is exactly what he had been doing in seeking to live the Christian life, Paul finally looked outside himself for help, owning up to his need for God,

> Oh, wretched man that I am! Who shall deliver me from the body of this death? (Rom. 7:24).

This cry is the apostle's admission that he needs help, that he cannot subdue the sin principle in his own strength. He calls out for deliverance from "the body of this death." This does not have reference to the body of flesh and blood in which we dwell, for it is neither good nor evil in itself. The "body of this death" is therefore fallen human nature, enslaved by sin and subject to death. The most sincere believer in Jesus Christ, if he seeks in his own strength to live a godly life, will find himself in the position of Paul's summary verse,

> . . . So, then, with the mind I myself serve the law of God; but with the flesh, the law of sin (Rom. 7:25).

Those who try by self-effort to overcome sin will experience constant defeat. With the inward regenerated self — "the law of the mind" — they will serve the law of God. However, with the old nature they will continue to be enslaved to the "law of sin."

Is there a way of victory? Is it possible for a person to be delivered from the tight grip of sin? Yes, triumph is possible! Conquest is within your grasp! "Who shall deliver me from the body of death?" the apostle cries, and immediately responds, "I thank God through Jesus Christ, our Lord" (Rom. 7:25). Deliverance from the power of sin can be known! Positive holiness in daily life can be experienced! It will not come, however, through our own feeble efforts to keep the law; but only by our reliance upon God. He came into the world in the person of His Son to be the sinner's substitute. Also, in the person of the Holy Spirit He enters the life of every believer, making that Christian's body a temple (I Cor. 6:19). The one who yields to the indwelling Holy Spirit receives power to defeat indwelling sin. This is the theme to be developed in Romans 8, the subject of our next three studies.

12

Victory and Sonship

Upon receiving the Lord Jesus as Savior some people immediately experience great joy, sweet peace, unruffled assurance, and victory over sin. Others, who just as sincerely trust Christ, endure periods of doubt and often feel defeated in their efforts to conquer sin. The joyous and victorious Christian must be careful not to judge his weaker brother, or be spiritually proud of himself. He must remember that all he is and has comes from God, and that he has an obligation to help his fellow Christian. Some find it much easier to be radiant and lovable than others. Many are blessed with a sound body, good looks, intelligence, a likable personality, and a natural ability to discipline themselves. Others must go through life suffering from the effects of poor health and unattractive appearance, with consequent feelings of inferiority or inadequacy. It is not easy for them to be radiant Christians. However, the eighth chapter of Romans has a message of instruction and hope for fearful and faltering saints. It does *not* tell believers that they will be free from problems, tears, disappointments, and failures, but shows how they can live *above* them. In this study, covering the first seventeen verses of Romans 8, believers are first of all assured of final victory, and secondly, instructed regarding the riches of their new relationship as sons of God.

I. TOTAL VICTORY ASSURED

The Christian who has an earnest desire for a joyous and godly life has the power available to him by which he can achieve this goal. He need not continue to be frustrated because of indwelling sin. The salvation of God provides deliverance, not only from guilt, but also from a life of abject servitude to sin.

A. *The Divine Liberation*

As Paul the apostle reflects upon this truth, a shout of triumph bursts from his lips. One cannot read these words without experiencing a thrill of joy.

> There is, therefore, now no condemnation to them who are in Christ Jesus . . . (Rom. 8:1).

Those who have placed their trust in Jesus Christ have been united to Him, and therefore are free from all blame. They have been removed from their old standing as guilty members of a fallen race, and are now "in Christ," the theme developed in Romans chapters 1-6. The joyous statement of Romans 8:1, however, goes far beyond that of judicial acquittal. It declares that believers in Christ have also been liberated from sin's slavery. According to Arndt & Gingrich, one of the finest Greek lexicons, *katakrima,* used here and translated "condemnation," means "the punishment following sentence." Believers redeemed from the guilt of sin are no longer doomed to a life of bondage to it. True, the "law of sin which is in my members" (Rom. 7:23), called by Paul in Romans 8:2 "the law of sin and death," is powerful, but the believer receives a new law or principle by which he is able to subdue it. This is the "law of the Spirit of life in Christ Jesus" (8:2). The *living* Spirit of God has entered the believer to overcome the death-dealing effect of indwelling sin.

The entrance of the Holy Spirit coincides with the believer's union with Christ through faith, for He is "the Spirit of life *in Christ*" (8:2). The defeat of sin and death, therefore, is based upon the redeeming activity of Jesus Christ. Paul says,

> For what the law could not do, in that it was weak through the flesh, God sending his own Son, in the likeness of sinful flesh and for sin, condemned sin in the flesh (Rom. 8:3).

Nowhere does Paul speak more carefully than in this verse. He declares that God, the Eternal Father, sent "his own Son," the second person of the Trinity, "in the likeness of sinful flesh," or, more literally, "in the likeness of flesh of sin." He does not say, "in the *likeness* of *flesh*," for that could be construed as a denial of our Lord's genuine humanity. Nor does Paul declare simply that the Lord came "*in flesh*," for this would not have conveyed the truth that Christ's incarnation involved participation in all the grief, temptation, and pain of a world under the curse of sin. Moreover, if the statement were that Jesus came "in *sinful* flesh," our Lord's absolute sinlessness would have been denied. The Eternal Son entered the human race, not in a garden of Eden untainted by the blight of sin, but in a world stained by immorality, cruelty, and hypocritical sham.

Christ also came *"for* sin"; that is, to deal with sin. His perfect life "in the likeness of flesh of sin" was the first time human nature had succeeded in resisting all temptation. His death was the means by which He took upon Himself the punishment mankind deserves, making it possible for God to remain just and yet save ungodly people. By His resurrection He broke the power of death, guaranteeing to all who trust Him that with Him they will live forever in a realm beyond the reach of sin. The phrase "condemned sin in the flesh" means that Jesus Christ in His humanity executed judicial sentence upon sin; that is, He both condemned sin and overthrew its power. In His "flesh" — His humanity — He met sin, defeated it, paid its price, and thus released His people from its guilt and enslavement.

The Lord Jesus did for us what the law cannot do. It passes sentence upon evil and shows men how they ought to live, but cannot give the believer the power he needs to overcome indwelling sin. This inability is not due to any fault in the law itself, but in the fact that weak human flesh is unable to meet its demands. Therefore, based on the fact that Jesus Christ dealt with sin, and through the power of the indwelling Holy Spirit, believers are enabled to fulfill the just requirement of the law.

> That the righteousness of the law might be fulfilled in us, who walk not after the flesh, but after the Spirit (Rom. 8:4).

The "righteous requirement" of the law is love for God and neighbor. The believer, no longer living "after the flesh," but under the control of the Spirit, is enabled to manifest true godliness in his daily walk.

B. *The Absolute Antithesis*

The next section, Romans 8:5-9, sets forth the absolute antithesis between a believer and an unbeliever. The person who lives "after the flesh," controlled and directed by his corrupt fallen nature, centers his thoughts and affection upon his own selfish interests. He seeks his own gratification. The one who walks "after the spirit" sets his mind upon the will of God and eternal realities.

> For they that are after the flesh do mind the things of the flesh; but they that are after the Spirit, the things of the Spirit (Rom. 8:5).

Paul goes on to say,

> For to be carnally minded is death, but to be spiritually minded is life and peace (Rom. 8:6).

The "mind of the flesh" as contrasted with the "mind of the Spirit," is death — estrangement from God. The sinner is not only on the way to eternal death, but is even now "dead in trespasses and sins" (Eph. 2:1). On the other hand, the "mind of the Spirit is *life* and *peace*," which are the antitheses of the *death* and the *misery* sin creates. In fact, this "mind of flesh" is actually at enmity with God. This hostility is displayed whenever men are aroused to a spirit of rebellion, upon coming face to face with God's righteous demands. Those who live under the control of indwelling sin therefore cannot please God, which is precisely what Paul says in Romans 8:7, 8.

> Because the carnal mind is enmity against God; for it is not subject to the law of God, neither, indeed, can be.
> So, then, they that are in the flesh cannot please God (Rom. 8:7, 8).

Believers, however, are assured that they are "in the Spirit," for He indwells everyone who trusts Christ. This is clearly indicated in I Corinthians 6:19, where Paul reminds the carnal Christians that their bodies are temples of the Holy Spirit. Here in Romans 8:9 he warns professing Christians, "Now if any man have not the Spirit of Christ, he is none of his." Every true believer can therefore be assured that he is not living "in the flesh," as a slave of the sin principle, but that he lives "in the Spirit." Christ has secured deliverance from the power of sin and death, and the Holy Spirit now lives within the believer, giving him both peace and victory.

C. *The Ultimate Goal*

Though a Christian possesses the Holy Spirit and no longer lives "after the flesh," he is still subject to temptation, has a sinful nature, and sometimes falls into evil thoughts, words and deeds. Although a recipient of eternal life, he nonetheless continues to experience pain and illness, and knows that someday he will die.

Recognizing that we might be discouraged when we reflect upon our present imperfections and the prospect of death, Paul assures us that though our bodies are mortal, the indwelling Holy Spirit is our guarantee of resurrection.

> But if the Spirit of him that raised up Jesus from the dead dwell in you, he that raised up Christ from the dead shall also give life to your mortal bodies by his Spirit that dwelleth in you (Rom. 8:11).

In summary, every believer can have the glorious certainty of total victory over sin. He has been united with the Lord Jesus Christ, who, by His life, death, resurrection and ascension, destroyed the power of sin and death. He has also received the indwelling Holy Spirit. Therefore he can increasingly suppress the power of sin in his daily life by walking in humble dependence upon the Holy Spirit, and can look forward to Heaven, where he shall be free from all the effects of sin.

II. DIVINE SONSHIP REALIZED

Paul now graphically depicts the new and thrilling thought that Christians are the sons and daughters of God, and sets forth some of the momentous implications of this truth for daily living. The concept of sonship is introduced by the exhortation,

> Therefore, brethren, we are debtors, not to the flesh, to live after the flesh.
> For if ye live after the flesh, ye shall die; but if ye, through the Spirit, do mortify the deeds of the body, ye shall live (Rom. 8:12, 13).

These verses are in perfect harmony with the doctrine of grace. Romans 8:13 does not affirm that salvation is acquired by works nor does it deny the security of a believer in Christ. Knowing that some who had professed Christ were not genuinely saved, the apostle declares the unchanging truth that living "after the flesh" leads to death. How can a person indwelt by the Holy Spirit, and delivered from the law of sin and death, live a life totally under the control of the flesh, from which he has been emancipated? The one who professes Christ but lives "after the flesh" does not possess true faith. Through the indwelling Spirit, the person who has received Jesus Christ will put to death the wicked deeds that indwelling sin seeks to perform through the body. A true believer will often be disappointed in his own conduct, and may even fall into deep sin, but, he will sincerely hate that sin, and desire victory over it. He will be successful to the extent he consciously yields himself to the indwelling Holy Spirit, and obeys the precepts of the New Testament. Even though he may sometimes fail, he is still assured that he is God's child.

> For as many as are led by the Spirit of God, they are the sons of God (Rom. 8:14).

A. *The Meaning of Sonship*

Believers are members of God's family through both regeneration and the judicial act of God. In the first epistle of John the emphasis of the Christian's sonship seems to be placed upon his spiritual birth, while in the writings of Paul the judicial or declarative aspect is emphasized. This distinction cannot be based upon the use of the word *tekna* (children) and *huios* (son), for they are often used interchangeably, and, in fact, Paul uses both words here in Romans 8. However, the apostle has reference to the truth that God takes people who were His enemies, enslaved to the sin principle, and makes them His children. He releases them from their former state of slavery, and gives them sonship with all its rights and privileges. For believers to live in servitude to indwelling sin, therefore, is totally incongruous.

> For ye have not received the spirit of bondage again to fear; but ye have received the Spirit of adoption, whereby we cry, Abba, Father (Rom. 8:15).

The Greek word rendered "adoption" means to be "placed as a son." Some Bible students believe Paul had in mind the Jewish custom of ceremonially giving a son status as a recognized heir at the age of twelve. Others believe the apostle has reference to adoption as we think of it today. In the first century, many Romans who had no sons of their own chose a boy to perpetuate their name and inherit their estate. Whether referring to Jewish or Roman custom, sonship here means release from servitude and the enjoyment of glorious freedom. Paul declares that when we were saved God did not give us the state of mind that belongs to slavery, but that which pertains to sonship. Therefore Christians know God as "Abba, Father." *Abba,* an Aramaic word, is the familiar term by which children in Hebrew-speaking families addressed their father.

B. *The Blessings of Sonship*

This concept of God as Father is unique to the Christian faith, and is a source of great comfort and strength to the believer. It gives a sense of God's loving concern for our needs, and reminds us that we are the objects of His tender affection. This sweet consciousness of divine sonship is the work of the Holy Spirit who indwells us. Paul declares,

> The Spirit himself beareth witness with our spirit, that we are the children of God (Rom. 8:16).

The Holy Spirit witnesses *"with* our spirit," not *"to* our spirit." As we believe God's Word and recognize the fact of our sonship, we instinctively cry, "Father," in response to our awareness of this filial relationship. The Spirit then comes with His witness to give us a deep inner consciousness that we are children of God. This witness is not a spectacular or highly emotional work, and is not something to seek through torturing oneself or agonizing in prayer. Rather, it comes to those who reflect upon God's Word and gratefully accept its truths.

The realization of sonship also assures the believer of eternal glory.

> And if children, then heirs — heirs of God, and joint heirs with Christ . . . (Rom. 8:17).

John also expressed this confidence when he said,

> Beloved, now are we the children of God, and it doth not yet appear what we shall be, but we know that, when he shall appear, we shall be like him; for we shall see him as he is (I John 3:2).

Christian friend, *you* are an heir of God. Glory awaits you! When your earthly pilgrimage is difficult and you become discouraged, reflect upon the great truths of the Gospel and believe them. God the Holy Spirit witnesses with your spirit, assuring you that you are indeed God's child, and that all is well. Eternal glory is your prospect.

13

Suffering and Glory

The spiritual growth of a Christian may be likened to the process that takes place in the physical realm as a baby matures to adulthood. The believer begins his spiritual existence as an infant member of God's family, and normally develops both in understanding and holiness. The rate at which this progress is made, however, varies with each person. Many spend a great portion of their Christian lives experiencing the frustrations and defeats described in Romans 7, while others continually radiate the joy and Christian graces of Romans 8. The road from earth to Heaven is never easy. Every believer faces opposition from indwelling sin, a hostile world, and the well-organized kingdom of Satan. Moreover, suffering and sorrow are present in every life. Paul is conscious of these things, and therefore encourages believers by telling them that the indwelling Holy Spirit is their guarantee of coming glory,

> . . . if so be that we suffer with him, that we may be also glorified together (Rom. 8:17).

To be a joint-heir with Christ in glory means to be a fellow-heir with Him in suffering. Because present affliction is a necessary prelude to glory, the apostle sets forth three great truths for all believers: (1) their glowing expectation; (2) their gracious support; and (3) their glorious confidence.

I. The Believer's Glowing Expectation

The Apostle Paul himself had recently passed through a time of great suffering. Less than two years earlier he had described the beatings, imprisonments, hardships, and dangers encountered in his service for Christ (II Cor. 11:23-33). He had also told of a severe physical affliction that had come upon him — the "thorn in the flesh" for which God had not granted removal (II Cor. 12:1-10). Yet the indomitable apostle could say,

> For I reckon that the sufferings of this present time are not worthy to be compared with the glory which shall be revealed in us (Rom. 8:18).

The Greek word *logizomai,* translated "I reckon," means "I make this judgment after careful deliberation." Living with a severe physical ailment, experiencing constant persecution, and being intimately acquainted with the hardships of imprisonments, beatings, and hunger, the apostle could still think of present suffering as only light and temporary in contrast to the eternal glory that awaits him. His words should be a source of great encouragement to every believer.

A. *The Realization of Creation's Yearning*

As the apostle thinks upon the afflictions of those who trust Christ, he comprehends the fact that the suffering of men stands in close relationship to the physical world. The created world is personified as eagerly awaiting the day when the children of God will be displayed in all their glory.

> For the earnest expectation of the creation waiteth for the manifestation of the sons of God (Rom. 8:19).

Phillips beautifully translated this verse, "The whole creation is on tiptoe to see the wonderful sight of the sons of God coming into their own." The entire natural world longs for the day when the children of God will receive their resurrection bodies. The apostle John had this in mind when he wrote,

> Beloved, now are we the children of God, and it doth not yet appear what we shall be, but we know that, when he shall appear, we shall be like him; for we shall see him as he is (I John 3:2).

The reason creation yearns for this revelation of the sons of God is because its own future is intricately bound up with that of man. The created world was subject to the curse because of man's sin. Nature itself is not responsible for the state of imperfection manifested in tornadoes, hurricanes, earthquakes, droughts and floods. Paul says this condition came upon the world "not willingly," for the sin of man is responsible for the imbalance of nature today. The apostle also declares that creation is "subject to vanity."

The word "vanity" may indicate that the earth system is enslaved to evil spiritual powers. As a result, men have tended to
worship the universe rather than the God who created it. Furthermore, God is the One who subjected the earth to vanity, placing
it under the curse. In doing so, however, He did not leave nature
without the hope of redemption.

> For the creation was made subject to vanity, not willingly
> but by reason of him who hath subjected the same in hope
> (Rom. 8:20).

Nature has been brought under the curse because of man's sin,
and will be restored to its pristine beauty when God manifests
His people in their glorified resurrection bodies.

> Because the creation itself also shall be delivered from the
> bondage of corruption into the glorious liberty of the children
> of God (Rom. 8:21).

This recovery of nature will take place in two stages.

First, during the millennial reign of Jesus Christ the whole
earth will share in the glory of its Lord, for ". . . the desert shall
rejoice, and blossom like the rose. It shall blossom abundantly,
and rejoice even with joy and singing" (Isa. 35:1, 2). Peace will
exist in the animal world, for "The wolf also shall dwell with the
lamb, and the leopard shall lie down with the kid; and the calf
and the young lion and the fatling together, and a little child
shall lead them. They shall not hurt nor destroy in all my holy
mountain" (Isa. 11:6, 9). Nations will live at peace with one
another, for men will "beat their swords into plowshares, and their
spears into pruning hooks; nation shall not lift up sword against
nation, neither shall they learn war any more" (Isa. 2:4). Great
topographical changes will take place on the face of the earth
(Zech. 14), and the land will be blessed with flowering gardens,
fruitful fields, and overflowing harvests. Glorified saints will be
ruling with Christ, for John in Revelation 20:4 declares,

> And I saw thrones, and they sat upon them, and judgment
> was given unto them; and I saw the souls of them that were
> beheaded for the witness of Jesus, and for the word of God,
> and who had not worshiped the beast, neither his image, nei-
> ther had received his mark upon their foreheads, or in their
> hands; and they lived and reigned with Christ a thousand years.

Wonderful as this time will be, however, it cannot equal the glory of eternity, because some sin will be present, some punishment will be required, and some will die. After Satan has led one final rebellion against God and His people, the material of our present universe will be purged and purified by fire, and out of this all-encompassing conflagration will emerge a new earth. The Heavenly Jerusalem will then descend to be the New Jerusalem, and the final vision of the apostle John will become reality.

> And I saw a new heaven and a new earth; for the first heaven and the first earth were passed away . . . (Rev. 21:1).

Sin shall never enter this gloriously transfigured new earth. At that time Paul's declaration, that "the creation itself also shall be delivered from the bondage of corruption into the glorious liberty of the children of God" (Rom. 8:21), will be fully realized.

B. *The Fulfillment of the Believer's Hope*

The apostle reminds his readers that the day for which creation longs has not yet arrived. He says,

> For we know that the whole creation groaneth and travaileth in pain together until now (Rom. 8:22).

This verse indicates that the sufferings of all creation, including mankind, are like the pangs of birth. In the midst of present affliction is the comforting expectation that a new age will soon be born. We who know Christ sometimes undergo deep agony while we wait for the day of resurrection and glory. However, even while we go through this period of waiting and suffering, we possess "the first fruits of the Spirit." The indwelling Holy Spirit is the "down payment" or "first installment" of the eternal glory that awaits us.

> And not only they, but ourselves also, who have the first fruits of the Spirit, even we ourselves groan within ourselves, waiting for the adoption, that is, the redemption of our body (Rom. 8:23).

The presence of the Holy Spirit, with the resultant change He has brought into the lives of those who have trusted Christ, is evidence that God is already working, and believers may be assured that the Lord always carries out that which He begins. The Holy Spirit has introduced us to the taste of Heaven.

> Once Heaven seemed a faroff place,
> Till Jesus showed His smiling face.
> Now it's begun within my soul;
> 'Twill last while endless ages roll.
> — *C. F. Butler*

Looking back upon what God has done in Christ, and considering all He is now doing through the indwelling Holy Spirit, believers can look forward with confidence to the day when they will be glorified. Therefore Paul concludes,

> But if we hope for that which we see not, then do we with patience wait for it (Rom. 8:25).

II. THE BELIEVER'S GRACIOUS SUPPORT

The afflicted Christian is strengthened not only by his expectation of glory to come, but also by the intercessory ministry of the indwelling Holy Spirit. True, the Lord Jesus prays for us in Heaven, but the Holy Spirit intercedes from within our souls. Many Christians are ignorant of the prayer-help of the indwelling Spirit.

> Likewise, the Spirit also helpeth our infirmity; for we know not what we should pray for as we ought; but the Spirit himself maketh intercession for us with groanings which cannot be uttered.
>
> And he that searcheth the hearts knoweth what is the mind of the Spirit, because he maketh intercession for the saints according to the will of God (Rom. 8:26, 27).

How difficult it is for us to concentrate on prayer or spiritual thoughts when our bodies are wracked with pain, or when our minds are numb with grief. Then, too, the enigma and mystery of suffering often perplexes us, so that we are unable to give specific reasons for certain difficult experiences. Many times, for example, we hardly know what or how we should pray when a loved one is ill. We are torn between our human desire and our knowledge that "to be with Christ . . . is far better" (Phil. 1:23). Nor are we certain whether or not it is God's will to heal. We are comforted to know that the Spirit gives us aid in our praying. When intense pain, deep grief, or our inability to know what is best hinders us from articulating specific requests, and we can only say in deep anguish, "Thy will be done," the Holy Spirit comes to our help. He presents our prayer before the throne of God. Since He is the third person of the Trinity and knows the

Father's will, He can express our prayer clearly and in acceptable form, so that we can be certain it will be heard and answered. All prayer is not necessarily phrased in beautiful human language, as the poet indicated when he wrote,

> Prayer is the soul's sincere desire,
> Unuttered or expressed,
> The motion of a hidden fire
> That trembles in the breast.
>
> Prayer is the burden of a sigh,
> The falling of a tear,
> The upward glancing of an eye,
> When none but God is near.
>
> — *J. Montgomery*

Christian friend, if you are dismayed when you do not know how to pray, remember, the indwelling Holy Spirit will take the deep inexpressible longings and aspirations of your heart and present them before the Father. You can be assured that God will grant you what is best.

III. THE BELIEVER'S GLORIOUS CONFIDENCE

Now the apostle is ready to establish the truth that life's trials are the means by which God accomplishes His loving purposes for His own. A superficial look at the difficulties and disappointments of life might lead us to think that God's plans are being frustrated, but the opposite is true. Therefore, though we may not fully understand our afflictions, and are unable to pray intelligently about them, we can know with absolute certainty that every trial and tear is part of an overall plan for our eternal good.

> And we know that all things work together for good to them that love God, to them who are the called according to his purpose.
> For whom he did foreknow, he also did predestinate to be conformed to the image of his Son, that he might be the firstborn among many brethren (Rom. 8:28, 29).

God's children have been foreknown by Him, and are the objects of His love. Everyone who has trusted Jesus Christ is predestinated someday to be sinlessly perfect like the Lord Jesus. The term "predestinate" means "to mark out the path beforehand." In God's blueprint, every believer has been designed for complete conformity to the image of His Son, so that Heaven will be populated by a multitude of Christlike saints. You may be certain that God's plans for you as His child will be fulfilled in every detail. His purposes, decreed from before the foundation of the world, are brought to realization here on earth. He calls men to salvation through His Word and Spirit, declares them righteous in Christ, and proceeds to glorify them.

> Moreover, whom he did predestinate, them he also called; and whom he called, them he also justified; and whom he justified, them he also glorified (Rom. 8:30).

Suffering plays an integral part in the process of spiritual growth in Christ, called sanctification, and its culmination will be perfect conformity to the Son of God. Those whom God has called and justified will inevitably be glorified.

Christians often find the hardships and difficulties of life to be unpleasant. Like everyone else, they wish they could avoid them. However, the Bible assures us that God has a program of suffering for His children by which He accomplishes purposes that can be realized in no other manner. The pain, disappointment, heartache and tears are unavoidable, but we can find great comfort in knowing that, for those who trust Christ, glory grows out of the suffering. Therefore, believers are never to rebel when the difficulties of life seem to be piling up. Encouraged by the prospect of coming glory, strengthened by the realization of the indwelling Holy Spirit's presence, sustained by His intercessory ministry, and fortified by the assurance that God is fulfilling His loving purpose, we should truly live above every circumstance. We can say with the apostle Paul,

> For our light affliction, which is but for a moment, worketh for us a far more exceeding and eternal weight of glory,
> While we look not at the things which are seen, but at the things which are not seen; for the things which are seen are temporal, but the things which are not seen are eternal (II Cor. 4:17, 18).

14

The Shout of Triumph

The Gospel is God's good news to sinners — a message of salvation, hope, and triumph. Believing on Jesus Christ brings acquittal from the guilt of sin, acceptance by God, freedom from legalistic self-effort, deliverance from the power of indwelling sin, and victory over suffering and death. The realization of salvation's fullness has prompted grateful Christians to compose and sing hundreds and thousands of praise-filled hymns. The joyful character of the gospel message is most vividly expressed in Romans 8:31-39. Here, in a shout of triumph, Paul extolls the glorious certainty of faith.

> What shall we then say to these things? If God be for us, who can be against us? (Rom. 8:31).

The apostle had just written of the believer's hope of perfection in Heaven, his gracious support through the indwelling Holy Spirit, and his wonderful assurance that God's loving purpose for each of His children will be realized. In the light of these marvelous truths, what is to be our response? Paul answers with the rhetorical question, "If God for us — who against us?" (literal translation). The "if" is not a term of uncertainty, but of presupposition, and really means "since." Yes, *God is for us.* God the Designer, Creator, Sustainer, Ruler, and Judge of the universe is *for us.* Since this is true, "Who can be against us?" Paul does not mean that we have no enemies. He knew, perhaps better than anyone else, the intensity of spiritual warfare against Satan and his hosts, and the bitterness of persecution at the hands of men who hated the Gospel. However, when a person knows that God is *for him,* he is also certain that no adversary will ultimately be able to harm him. When God is *for us,* all things work together for our good.

The believer's salvation is full, rich, and permanent. God will never set aside His verdict of acquittal, rescinding the salvation He has bestowed. Moreover, separation from Christ's love is an utter impossibility, for nothing in all the universe can break the bond between Christ and His own.

I. Annulment of Salvation Inconceivable

The apostle visualizes a courtroom over which God presides as Judge. The Christian, obviously a member of Adam's sinful race by natural birth, is acquitted of all guilt, and declared righteous because of his faith in the Lord Jesus. Will anyone dare come forward to make an allegation against this believer? Will any condemn? Shall any stand before the Supreme Arbiter to accuse those whom He has declared righteous?

> Who shall lay any thing to the charge of God's elect? . . . Who is he that condemneth? . . . (Rom. 8:33, 34).

The implied answer is, "No one dares challenge God's declaration." The basis for the apostle's confidence is expressed in verses 32 and 33. God, in giving His Son, has provided abundant proof of His changeless love, and Jesus Christ now lives in glorious resurrection power to intercede for His own.

A. *God's Proven Love*

Every Christian knows that the supreme demonstration of God's love is found in Christ.

> For God so loved the world, that he gave his only begotten Son, that whosoever believeth in him should not perish, but have everlasting life (John 3:16).

Though multitudes can quote this Bible verse from memory, no one can fully fathom its depths, or understand how much it pained the Heavenly Father to send His Son. With the unfathomable cost of our salvation in mind, Paul declares,

> He that spared not his own Son, but delivered him up for us all, how shall he not with him also freely give us all things? (Rom. 8:32).

The words "spared not His own Son" bring to mind the story recorded in Genesis 22. God tested Abraham's faith by saying to him, "Take now thy son, thine only son Isaac, whom thou lovest

... and offer him ... for a burnt offering upon one of the mountains which I will tell thee of" (Gen. 22:2). Abraham was puzzled, but in obedience he traveled to the apointed place of sacrifice with Isaac. Only after the young man had been bound to the altar, and when Abraham had raised his knife, did God intervene. He commended the aged patriarch, saying, "Thou hast not withheld thy son, thine only son from me" (Gen. 22:12). In the Septuagint, with which Paul was well acquainted, the same Greek word translated "withheld" in this verse is used by Paul in Romans 8:32, and rendered "spared." Even as Abraham did not "withhold" his beloved son Isaac, so God did not "withhold" *His* Son, the second person of the Trinity. Reflecting upon the thoughts and feelings of Abraham as he went up the mountain of sacrifice with Isaac, we gain some understanding of what it meant for God to give His Son.

In another sense, God did not "spare" His Son. Speaking prophetically, Isaiah had declared, "It pleased the Lord to bruise him; he hath put him to grief" (Isa. 53:10). This does not mean that God found pleasure in the suffering of Christ, but that He chose this shameful death for His Son because it was the only way He could provide redemption for sinners. When the Lord Jesus went to the cross, the Father "made him, who knew no sin, to be sin for us; that we might be made the righteousness of God in him" (II Cor. 5:21). How unworthy we are of such love!

God also "delivered him up for us all." He turned over His Son to Satan the archenemy and to wicked men. Jesus demonstrated His understanding of this while in the Garden of Gethsemane, for He said to the company who had come to arrest Him, "This is your hour, and the power of darkness" (Luke 22:53). God allowed Satan and the forces of evil to vent upon His Son all their malignity and hatred. He delivered the Lord Jesus up to gainsaying, mocking, scourging, spitting, and crucifixion at the hands of wicked men. More than a century ago, one of God's servants wrote, "Who delivered up Jesus to die? Not Judas, for money; not Pilate, for fear; not the Jews, for envy — but the Father, for love!"

God's love is beyond description! The Almighty is *for us!* Since God has done this, will He not also meet our needs day by day? Will He who has done so much for us in the past forsake us now? Of course not! We can be absolutely certain that God shall "freely give us all things." The One whose love prompted Him to give His Son to the shame and pain of Calvary does not change.

B. *Christ's Present Life*

The permanency of the believer's salvation assured, the apostle now calls their attention to Christ, their living and exalted Savior. He mentions His death and resurrection, but places emphasis upon His present activity.

> . . . [It is] Christ that died, yea rather, that is risen again, who is even at the right hand of God, who also maketh intercession for us? (Rom. 8:34).

The Savior who died for us and rose again is now in His glorified human body at the Father's right hand. The Lord Jesus has not forgotten us. Christian friend, He still loves you, knows your needs, and intercedes on your behalf. He understands you, for, although He never sinned, He himself was "tested in all points" like you are. His love for you has not diminished one iota. He is neither defective in character nor in spiritual perception, and His prayers for you will be answered. This intercessory ministry of the living Christ is another guarantee that God will never change the verdict by which He declared you justified. You will never lose your salvation.

II. SEPARATION FROM CHRIST'S LOVE IMPOSSIBLE

Having spoken of Jesus Christ in His death, resurrection, ascension, and present ministry of intercession, the apostle asks another question, this one having to do with Christ's love (Rom. 8:35).

A. *Christ's Love — Endures Through All Circumstances*

The apostle names one environmental peril after another to state emphatically that no distressing situation or combination of difficulties can take away the love of Christ from the believer.

> What shall separate us from the love of Christ? Shall tribulation, or distress, or persecution, or famine, or nakedness, or peril, or sword? (Rom. 8:35).

Trials are not a sign that Christ's love has been withdrawn. The people of God have always suffered for their faith, and have emerged victorious in the end. Quoting Psalm 44:22 for our encouragement, the apostle declares,

> . . . for thy sake we are killed all the day long, we are accounted as sheep for the slaughter (Rom. 8:36).

Believers should not merely endure suffering with stoicism, passively submitting to the inevitable. Instead, they are to realize that they are winning a most glorious victory. Even when living in the midst of conditions most people would term intolerable, Christians are able to rejoice in the knowledge that the blessings of eternity will far outweigh the sufferings of earth's brief time. Therefore Paul exclaims,

> Nay, in all these things we are more than conquerors (literally, "super-conquerors") through him that loved us (Rom. 8: 37).

Christian friend, the world may seem to be tumbling in about you. You may be heartsick and lonely, discouraged and bewildered, physically weak and miserable. However, remember that Christ's love endures. He knows, He cares, and He intercedes for you. His love will never change. Therefore you may be assured that your distress is only temporary, and that your present suffering is light compared to the glory that will someday be yours.

B. *Divine Love — Overcomes All Enemies*

Every adversary that one could imagine is powerless to separate the believer from God's love. The apostle soars to the pinnacle of Christian experience as he jubilates,

> For I am persuaded that neither death, nor life, nor angels, nor principalities, nor powers, nor things present, nor things to come,
> Nor height, nor depth, nor any other creation, shall be able to separate us from the love of God, which is in Christ Jesus, our Lord (Rom. 8:38, 39).

Note the words, "I am persuaded." This is the expression of deep, Spirit-produced, inner assurance. The apostle is not setting forth a mere theory, or engaging in a display of rhetoric. He has experienced tribulation, distress, nakedness, peril, and sword, but these seeming catastrophes could not separate him from the consciousness of Christ's love. In fact, they have brought the Lord Jesus closer. Therefore, Paul ransacks God's universe for powers that might be hostile to the Christian, and declares his absolute certainty that nothing in Heaven above, in earth beneath, or under the earth, whether in time or in eternity, can separate the believer from the love of God in Christ.

1. "Neither death nor life"

Death and life are both powerless to harm eternally the one who has trusted Jesus Christ. The Lord Himself died, and by His resurrection destroyed death's power. For the believer, to die is simply to depart this life and be with Christ (Phil. 1:21, 23; II Cor. 5:6-8). Life is mentioned here as the antithesis of death. It is often easier to die than to live, but the most trying experiences of life are unable to break the bond of love between God and us.

2. "Nor angels, nor principalities, nor powers"

The words, "nor angels, nor principalities, nor powers," refer to supernatural beings — both good and evil. The holy angels, of course, would not seek to harm us, but Paul is speaking hypothetically. The organized kingdom of Satan with its principalities and powers has already been conquered by Jesus Christ, for, "When he ascended up on high, he led captivity captive" (Eph. 4:8), and, "having spoiled principalities and powers, he made a show of them openly, triumphing over them . . ." (Col. 2:15). They are defeated foes.

3. "Nor things present, nor things to come"

The next grouping, "nor things present, nor things to come," refers to the dimensions of time. Even after the present planetary system has been burned with fire and the new heavens and earth appear, the same unchanging God who loved us through Christ will still be the universal Sovereign. He is the Lord of time and eternity.

4. "Nor height, nor depth"

The words, "nor height, nor depth," are taken by many Bible students to be a declaration that nothing in the expanses of space can bring real harm to the child of God. While this is undoubtedly true, it is possible that Paul uses these words as the astrologers of his day. For them, the term "height" (*hupsoma*) indicated the time a star was at its zenith, when its influence was greatest, and "depth" (*bathos*) referred to a star at its lowest point. Paul declares that believers need not fear that the stars in their movement can bring harm. The Christian living under the care of his Heavenly Father is in no way the victim of blind fate.

5.   "Nor any other creation"

The last words, "nor any other creation," leave absolutely no possible loophole. Nothing in all the universe — absolutely nothing, neither in this world, nor in some other entirely different realm men might discover — can separate us from God's love in Christ.

Friend, God's love for you has been proven. It will never change. It endures through life's most distressing circumstances, and is so great that all the terrifying forces and hostile powers in the world cannot overcome it. Since this is true, why should you be afraid? God has predestinated you to be like His Son Jesus Christ. He will not let anything frustrate this loving purpose for you. Your salvation is secure. He loved you when you were a sinner and completely unlovely.

> Herein is love, not that we loved God, but that he loved us, and sent his Son to be the propitiation for our sins (I John 4:10).

God will always love you, for "God is love." He has accepted you in Christ, has made you a member of His family, and will own you as His forever.

15

The Sovereignty of God

No chapter in the Bible has had more divergence of interpretation, or undergone more criticism, than Romans 9. Some Bible scholars believe it teaches that God arbitrarily predestines men to either Heaven or Hell. Others, maintaining that God is not capricious and that man is free, rational, and morally responsible, hold that this chapter in no way teaches a predetermined reprobation to Hell. Actually, the controversy is altogether unnecessary, for the apostle is not dealing primarily with the subject of foreknowledge and election to salvation, but with the so-called "Jewish question." Hebrew believers were confused by the fact that in the Church there was no distinction between Israelite and Gentile. At the same time, Judaistic critics charged that if God had turned from His covenant with Israel, He was guilty of breaking His promises to them.

As the apostle initiates his defense of God's right to set aside the nation of Israel for a time, he reflects upon the unbelief they had displayed toward the Gospel and he is deeply stirred. Knowing that some of his Judaistic adversaries have accused him of insincerity and disloyalty, he vehemently defends his veracity and patriotism.

> I say the truth in Christ, I lie not, my conscience also bearing me witness in the Holy Spirit,
> That I have great heaviness and continual sorrow in my heart.
> For I could wish that I myself were accursed from Christ for my brethren, my kinsmen according to the flesh (Rom. 9: 1-3).

Paul knew that nothing could separate him from the love of Christ, but because of his intense devotion to his nation he uses the language of an unattainable desire and declares that he "*could* wish himself accursed from Christ" for the sake of his people. He proceeds to point out that God's sovereign *favor* has been displayed toward Israel, and His sovereign *freedom* has been exercised throughout history.

I. God's Sovereign Favor Displayed

Israel, as God's chosen nation, enjoyed eight unique spiritual privileges.

> . . . to whom pertaineth the *adoption,* and the *glory,* and the *covenants,* and the giving of the *law,* and the *service* of God, and the *promises;*
>
> Whose are the *fathers,* and of whom, as concerning the flesh, *Christ* came, who is over all, God blessed forever. Amen (Rom. 9:4, 5).

Adoption is God's gracious establishment of a filial relationship between the Jewish nation and Himself. Israel is collectively named the "son of God" in Exodus 4:22, which reads, "Thus saith the LORD, Israel is my son, even my firstborn." God also declares in Hosea 11:1, "When Israel was a child, then I loved him, and called my son out of Egypt." The Jewish nation alone had this unique father-son kinship with God.

The next privilege Paul mentions is the *glory* — the manifested presence of God. When Israel left Egypt, the Lord led them by a cloud during the day and a pillar of fire by night. At the time of the giving of the law at Mount Sinai, Moses records, "the sight of the glory of the LORD was like devouring fire on the top of the mount" (Exod. 24:17). This same brightness covered and filled the tabernacle (Exod. 40:34-38), appeared upon the mercy seat in the holy of holies (Lev. 16:2), and filled the temple (I Kings 8:10, 11). This glowing sign gave proof to Israel that God dwelt with them, met them in worship, and led them against their enemies.

Thirdly, Israel received the *covenants*. God promised Abraham the land of Canaan as an everlasting possession (Gen. 12; 15; 22). Furthermore, He assured David that He would preserve his lineage and give him a physical descendant who would occupy his throne forever (II Sam. 7:13). God also spoke of a "new covenant" He would make with Israel, saying to them ". . . [I] will bring you into your own land. . . . I will take away the stony heart out of your flesh, and I will give you an heart of flesh. And I will put my Spirit within you, and cause you to walk in my statutes, and ye shall keep mine ordinances, and do them" (Ezek.

36:24, 26, 27). No other nation has entered into such special covenant relationship with God.

The fourth privilege of Israel was the custodianship of the *law* given at Mount Sinai; the fifth, the unique *service* of the tabernacle and temple; sixth, the salvation and kingdom *promises*; seventh, the possession of a history featuring the *fathers,* men of God like Abraham, Isaac, Jacob, Moses, and David. Finally, the crowning fact that *Christ,* the One called "the mighty God" in Isaiah 9:6, and whom Paul says "is over all, God blessed forever," derived His humanity from Mary, a descendant of David. Deep anguish gripped the apostle because the nation he loved so much, this people who had received such signal favors from God, continued in unbelief. In our day of violent anti-Semitism, however, mankind must be reminded that Israel, in spite of her continuing unbelief, is destined to return to God, and will enjoy a place of worldwide prominence and leadership.

II. GOD'S SOVEREIGN FREEDOM EXERCISED

Having shown that Israel is indeed God's elect nation, the apostle anticipates an objection. Some will be unable to harmonize Israel's spiritual priority with the equality of Jew and Gentile in the Church. What about the many promises made to national Israel? Will God break them? Paul positively asserts that the Lord's word will stand!

> Not as though the word of God hath taken no effect . . . (Rom. 9:6).

The apostle next demonstrates God's sovereign right to grant the fulfillment of the promised blessings only to those natural descendants of Jacob whom He chooses; that is, to those who meet His spiritual qualifications. Not all the posterity of the patriarchs are Israelites in the true sense of the word. The apostle illustrates this by appealing to certain well-known facts from Israel's history.

A. *In His Choice of Isaac*

Every Israelite knew that Ishmael was the son of Abraham and Hagar, and that Keturah bore Abraham six sons. However, though these descendants received certain blessings and inheritances, they were not included in the spiritual privileges of the covenant granted to Isaac. The Lord did not exclude Ishmael and the sons of Keturah from the possibility of salvation through

faith, but He did set them aside in separate national groups without unique spiritual rights. God chose to carry out His special
covenant promises to Abraham through Isaac, the supernaturally
conceived son of Sarah — "in Isaac shall thy seed be called"
(Rom. 9:7, quoted from Gen. 21:12). This illustration shows
that faith, not heredity, is the eternal principle of sonship. Therefore Paul concludes,

> . . . They who are the children of the flesh, these are not
> the children of God, but the children of the promise are
> counted as the seed (Rom. 9:8).

These "children of promise" are those who, like Abraham, believe God. In the bestowment of spiritual blessings, the Lord op-
erates on the principle of faith rather than mere national descent.
Therefore, He has a sovereign right to postpone the fulfillment
of His promises to Israel as long as the nation continues in unbelief.

B. *In His Choice of Jacob*

Next, Paul refers to the well-known story of Jacob and Esau to
emphasize God's sovereign freedom and righteousness.

> And not only this, but when Rebecca also had conceived by
> one, even by our father, Isaac
> (For the children being not yet born, neither having done
> any good or evil, that the purpose of God according to elec-
> tion might stand, not of works, but of him that calleth),
> It was said unto her, The elder shall serve the younger.
> As it is written, Jacob have I loved, but Esau have I hated
> (Rom. 9:10-13).

Here were two boys, having the same parents, and conceived at
the same time; yet the younger was chosen from before his birth
to a place of spiritual priority over the elder. God made this
choice before Jacob had demonstrated faith or any other spiritual
quality. He determined to make Jacob, not Esau, the channel
through whom He would work out His covenant promises and
bring salvation to mankind.

The words "the elder shall serve the younger" refer to Israel
and Edom, the nations that descended from Jacob and Esau,
rather than to the men themselves. (The Edomites on several
occasions served as slaves of the Israelites.) Moreover, the phrase
"Jacob have I loved, but Esau have I hated," in keeping with the

accepted usage of the day, indicates that God saw fit to honor Jacob and his descendants over Esau. The offspring of Jacob, not Esau, became the vehicles to whom the Lord spoke His oracles and through whom He made known His truth.

We must remember also that the election referred to in Romans 9:10-13 is not a choice for eternal salvation or perdition, but God's predetermining of the role that individuals and nations would play in this earthly life. Salvation was available for Esau and any of his descendants willing to believe God. However, the land of Canaan, the law, the tabernacle and temple service, and the yet unrealized promises of national blessing and priority — these were reserved for Jacob and his posterity.

God's right to make this choice was readily acknowledged by every Israelite. Using the same logic, he would be forced to admit that even as God had the prerogative to make this determination, so He could with absolute propriety postpone the full realization of His promises to the nation of Israel. The mere fact that the Jews were descendants of Jacob did not guarantee them immunity from judgment.

C. *In His Dealing With Israel and Pharaoh*

The third illustration of God's right to exercise freely His sovereign will involves Israel and Pharaoh. The Lord showed mercy to the undeserving nation of Israel, but through judgment made an object lesson of Pharaoh. Israel's grievous sin in making and worshiping a golden calf, thus imitating the vile idolatry of the Canaanites, deserved dire punishment, but God in mercy withheld it. Shortly after this event, Moses, with the memory of his people's sin still fresh in his mind, asked the Lord, "Show me thy glory" (Exod. 33:18). Before answering this request, God declared to Moses the words quoted in Romans 9:15,

> . . . I will have mercy on whom I will have mercy, and I will have compassion on whom I will have compassion.

Israel had no right to claim God's mercy, but the Lord graciously displayed His longsuffering and patience. Paul therefore concludes,

> So, then, it is not of him that willeth, nor of him that runneth, but of God that showeth mercy (Rom. 9:16).

Pharaoh, on the other hand, tasted God's righteous wrath. This Egyptian king had been treating the Israelites, who were his slaves, in a cruel and heartless manner. When Moses came to him with God's demand that he allow the Israelites to leave, the obstinate monarch refused. As God through Moses and Aaron began to work miracles of judgment upon the Egyptian people, Pharaoh became more determined than ever not to release the children of Israel. A careful reading of the historical account in Exodus 7 through 11 indicates that Pharaoh's moral character degenerated as he stubbornly resisted what he knew to be God's will. Therefore, God cannot be charged with acting arbitrarily or with making Pharaoh a mere pawn on the chessboard of fate. God had the unquestioned right to place him as king of Egypt at this crucial time, and to make him an object lesson demonstrating what happens to one who stubbornly resists the Almighty. This is what the apostle means when he says,

> For the scripture saith unto Pharaoh, Even for this same purpose have I raised thee up, that I might show my power in thee, and that my name might be declared throughout all the earth (Rom. 9:17).

God is not acting unjustly when He shows mercy to undeserving people as He did to Israel, or displays His wrath as He did with Pharaoh.

> Therefore hath he mercy on whom he will have mercy, and whom he will he hardeneth (Rom. 9:18).

D. *In Vessels of Wrath and Mercy*

Though the Sovereign God had been longsuffering with Pharaoh, He nevertheless had not dealt with him as mercifully as with Israel. Therefore Paul imagines his opponents saying,

> . . . Why doth he yet find fault? For who hath resisted his will? (Rom. 9:19).

The apostle replies by declaring that even as the clay cannot question the potter's choice to make it a vessel that will serve some lowly purpose, so man had no right to call God to account. A potter has the right to design one vessel for ornamental purposes and another as a container for refuse, and God has a right to give some people more privileges and opportunities than others. It was God's prerogative to act in judgment when Pharaoh continued his obstinacy, but to withhold punishment from Israel. He had been patient with Pharaoh, but finally used him as an example of His wrath and power. Pharaoh, through a combination of his own willful desires, a set of circumstances, and the subsequent hardening action of God, became "a vessel of wrath fitted to destruction" (Rom. 9:22).

The apostle now digresses from the subject of God's sovereign choice of people for earthly privilege and introduces the concept of eternal salvation. He declares that God has a right to hold back judgment and show special favor to those He has predestined for glory.

> And that he might make known the riches of his glory on the vessels of mercy, which he had before prepared unto glory,
> Even us, whom he hath called, not of the Jews only, but also of the Gentiles? (Rom. 9:23, 24).

These vessels of mercy are they, both Jew and Gentile, who have placed their trust in Jesus Christ.

The apostle has developed a striking parallel. Even as God was long-suffering with Pharaoh, so He has been patient with Israel. Even as Pharaoh's stubborn refusal to do the will of God furnished the occasion for the Lord to demonstrate His power and declare His name throughout the earth, so Israel's defiant unbelief has provided the setting for God to display the riches of His glory in saving those who believe in Christ. The Lord has been long-suffering with the nation of Israel but now temporarily puts her aside as "a vessel of wrath." He does this to display His mercy to those who will believe.

To summarize, then, Romans 9 clearly declares God's sovereignty and righteousness. For reasons we cannot question, the Lord chose to show special mercy to Israel. He determined that He would channel salvation blessings to all mankind through Abraham, Isaac, Jacob, and their descendants, the nation of Israel. In setting aside Ishmael, the sons of Keturah, and Esau, He did not arbitrarily exclude them from the possibility of eternal salvation. Furthermore, though He showed mercy to undeserving Israel, He did not necessarily have to treat Pharaoh in precisely the same manner. Still, God did not deal with this wicked king arbitrarily. Of his own volition, Pharaoh determined to oppose God, and the Lord was perfectly just in using him as a vehicle for the display of His wrath and power. Similarly, God as the divine potter has the right to design and make some vessels for more exalted functions than others. He had the prerogative to exalt Israel, and now He cannot be questioned when He temporarily sets her aside. Therefore, in this dispensation of grace, He makes no distinction between Jew and Gentile, but extends His mercy to all who believe the Gospel of Jesus Christ.

Friend, do not take the despairing view that you have been predetermined to eternal perdition. The Bible nowhere indicates that God has predestined anyone for everlasting destruction. Your life is not under the control of a vengeful deity or blind fate. You are a morally responsible being, created in the image and likeness of God, and the object of His love. Believe on Jesus Christ today, and join the company God has ordained to enjoy the beauty and blessing of eternity in Heaven.

16

Israel's Unbelief

The Bible clearly teaches that God is in control of the universe, that He directs the affairs of men to certain predetermined goals, and that He even permits evil to play a part in His overall program. Romans 9 vindicates this sovereign freedom of God. The Creator is a living, loving, purposeful Being, not a blind, heartless, inexorable Fate "which dooms to slow decay or sudden death, and to eternal oblivion all that is great, good and beautiful in this world."

Instead, He made man in His own image, loves him, and desires fellowship with him. People are not "but helpless pieces of the game He plays upon His checkerboard of nights and days," but imagebearers of God who can achieve true satisfaction only through a life in harmony with God's will. The Lord's freedom and sovereignty in no way infringe upon man's moral responsibility. Paul declares that men are lost not by divine decree, but because they find the Gospel offensive, and therefore they deliberately misinterpret and reject it.

I. The Offense of the Cross

The Gospel is most offensive to some people because it deals a devastating blow to human pride, and it precludes all rival religious systems.

A. *Its Destruction of Human Pride*

Men have always wanted to believe that they could build a ladder to Heaven by their own good deeds. Some have fancied themselves to be morally worthy of eternal life on the basis of their conduct. Others have looked to the faithful observance of religious ritual as the means to ensure their entrance into Glory. This idea of a "works-achieved" salvation is in direct contrast to the Gospel, which declares that every person possesses a sinful nature and therefore his best deeds are tainted and imperfect. Furthermore, everyone stands guilty before God and is in need of forgiveness, which is available only through faith in Jesus Christ. This denial of man's ability to earn salvation is especially distasteful to the self-righteous religionist. For this reason, extremely scrupulous people have often rejected the Gospel, whereas the erstwhile wicked and godless have embraced it.

When the Good News was preached during the first century, many Gentiles who had never shown any interest in obtaining righteousness, believed the message of salvation; but the Jews, who had strenuously sought to obtain righteousness before God, did not achieve it (Rom. 9:30, 31). The reason so many failed to experience genuine forgiveness and peace is stated by the apostle:

> Why? Because they sought it not by faith but, as it were, by the works of the law. For they stumbled at that stumbling stone;
> As it is written, Behold, I lay in Zion a stumbling stone and rock of offense; and whosoever believeth on him shall not be ashamed (Rom. 9:32, 33).

Paul brings together the words of Isaiah 8:14 and 28:16, in which the Lord promised Israel that during the approaching Assyrian invasion He would be a "sanctuary," providing safety for those who will trust Him, and a "rock" upon which they will be able to stand secure and not be ashamed. However, God warned those who trusted in pagan deities, or in their treaties with heathen neighbors, that He would be a destructive obstacle to them — "a stone of stumbling" and a "rock of offense." Applying these words to his readers, Paul declares that Jesus Christ has become "a stone of stumbling" to the majority of the Jews. He uses the Greek word *skandalon,* which means "to be offended by," or "annoyed with." This message of a crucified Savior, and the teaching that they were sinners on the same spiritual level as the pagans, aroused their antagonism. The apostle, however, assures believers that their trust will not prove to be ill-founded. Men may ridicule the message that proclaims a Savior who died vicariously for the sins of His people, but a glorious day of vindication will come for every true believer in Christ.

B. *Its Demand for a New Loyalty*

Having shown that the message of the cross is offensive to religionists because it humbles them, the apostle proceeds to point out that the Gospel is also objectionable to them because of its totalitarian demands. Faith in Christ cannot be a mere adjunct to existing religious form or ritual, but must include a renouncement of their former methods of seeking to gain favor with God. During the apostolic period, many adherents of Judaism, upon turning to Christ, found this demand extremely difficult to obey. Paul, himself a strict Pharisee before his conversion to Christ, understands their problem. He recalls vividly his own strong loyalty to Judaism and the deep feelings that drove him on in his early efforts to destroy the Church. He remembers too how he had kicked against the goads and bruised himself upon the "stone of stumbling" until the day he surrendered to Jesus Christ. Therefore, he expresses his heartfelt, deep-seated concern for his people, acknowledges their earnestness, but declares sadly that they are attempting to be right with God by wrong methods.

> Brethren, my heart's desire and prayer to God for Israel is, that they might be saved.
>
> For I bear them witness that they have a zeal for God, but not according to knowledge.
>
> For they, being ignorant of God's righteousness, and going about to establish their own righteousness, have not submitted themselves unto the righteousness of God (Rom. 10:1-3).

Israel had been seeking to *earn* salvation through works, instead of recognizing that God graciously *bestows* forgiveness and acceptance upon those who trust Him. By this they showed that they completely misunderstood the real meaning of the law. The Mosaic code was intended by God to reveal man's deep sinfulness, his utter helplessness to obey God perfectly, and his need for God's gracious forgiveness, but the religious leaders had developed it into a works-system designed to earn salvation.

Furthermore, having hurt themselves at the "stone of stumbling" (Christ), the people of Israel were guilty of setting their wills against God, refusing to subject themselves to His plan. Their intense loyalty to the "traditions of the fathers" became a strong hindrance to their acceptance of Jesus Christ. This rejection of Christ was a tragic mistake, made against overwhelming evidence. As they continued to oppose the Gospel, in spite of the undeniable fact that Jesus Christ conquered death, and the incontrovertible evidence in the lives of transformed believers, they increased in blindness and in hostility to Christ and His followers.

II. The Simplicity of the Gospel

The apostle hastens to make clear that though his countrymen were ignorant of God's righteousness, this lack of knowledge is no excuse. His people were guilty of resisting God, as indicated in Romans 10:3, where he asserts that they "have not *submitted themselves* unto the righteousness of God." Moreover, Israel's unbelief could not be excused by the claim that they were not able to understand the Gospel because of its complicated nature. In fact, Paul clearly points out that the Good News of Christ presents salvation far more simply than the law. The Gospel removes the old pressure of the legal code, puts an end to its veil of obscurity, and rescinds its restrictive barriers.

A. *The Old Tension Removed*

The believer is not under the jurisdiction of the Mosaic system.

> For Christ is the end of the law for righteousness to every-one that believeth (Rom. 10:4).

The Greek word *telos* translated "end," expresses the combined thought of "goal" and "termination."

Christ is the *goal* toward which the law aimed when it set forth God's holy demands that men could not obey because of their sinful nature. The sin and trespass offerings were provided to restore the sinner to fellowship with God, for they pointed to Jesus Christ and the sacrifice He would someday provide. He is also the *termination* of the law, since with His death the whole Levitical system was fulfilled, as signified by the rending of the veil in the Temple.

Paul declares that New Testament salvation is more easily understood and provides more freedom than that of the preceding dispensations. He does this by pointing out first of all that Old Testament believers lived under the burden of a scrupulous obedience to a multitude of minute rules and regulations. Quoting from Leviticus 18:5, he says,

> For Moses describeth the righteousness which is of the law, that the man who doeth those things shall live by them (Rom. 10:5).

Though many of the religionists took this as a legalistic means of earning eternal life, and considered themselves certain of a "works-achieved" salvation, the true Old Testament believer knew that he needed God's grace. However, he did feel the pressure of the law's demands, and earnestly sought to comply with them. Faithfully presenting his offerings, he believed that God in grace forgave his sins. Therefore, though he experienced real salvation and a measure of true fellowship with God, he was in constant tension for he lived under a system that demanded an obedience he could not render, and made provision for sacrifices which he offered but did not fully understand. When Christ came as our substitute, He first kept the law perfectly, and then on the cross paid the price for human sin, thus ending forever the claim of the law upon all those who believe on Him.

B. *The Old Obscurity Ended*

Paul further explains the simplicity and accessibility of the Gospel by quoting from Deuteronomy 30:12-14, interspersing his own comments.

> But the righteousness which is of faith speaketh on this wise, Say not in thine heart, Who shall ascend into heaven? (that is, to bring Christ down from above);
> Or, Who shall descend into the deep? (that is, to bring up Christ again from the dead).
> But what saith it? The word is near thee, even in thy mouth, and in thy heart; that is, the word of faith, which we preach (Rom. 10:6-8).

Moses uttered these words in their original form to Israel shortly before his death. He assured his people that God's commands were understandable, practical, and available. They did not need to ascend to Heaven or go to the utmost parts of the sea to find God's laws, for the Lord has given them to Moses and Israel in turn had learned them and could repeat them. Of course, Moses was not speaking legalistically as if they could merit Heaven by their own obedience, but asserting that through their sincere efforts to keep these laws, and through the faith-prompted presentation of their sacrifices, they could experience real fellowship with God.

Paul sees in these words an emphasis upon faith — even though it is somewhat obscure because of the nature of the law as a system of types and shadows — and quotes them to show that in the dispensation of grace the object of faith (Christ) is far clearer. He points to the incarnation and resurrection of the Lord Jesus, saying, "Do not say to yourself, 'Who will go up to

Heaven?' (that is, to bring Christ down, as though He had never become incarnate and lived on earth). Do not say, 'Who will go down to the abyss?' (that is, to bring Christ back from the dead as if He had not already been resurrected)." In Jesus Christ, God's salvation is near us. We need not look to Heaven for some miraculous sign, nor to the departed dead for answers to the mysteries of the hereafter. Through the living Christ, who came from Heaven and conquered death, salvation is here, present, and available. The word of the Gospel is,

> That if thou shalt confess with thy mouth the Lord Jesus, and shalt believe in thine heart that God hath raised him from the dead, thou shalt be saved.
> For with the heart man believeth unto righteousness; and with the mouth confession is made unto salvation (Rom. 10: 9, 10).

The fact that in the tenth verse the apostle mentions faith first, and then confession, shows that he did not intend the ninth verse to teach that a person may confess Jesus as Lord before believing on Him in his heart. Obviously there can be no genuine confession without real belief in the heart.

Furthermore, when Paul says, "With the heart man believeth unto *righteousness;* and with the mouth confession is made unto *salvation,"* he is not indicating that righteousness and salvation are different entities. Faith is the means by which God imputes righteousness to us, declares us guiltless, and accepts us into His favor. The term "salvation," however, is a bit broader in its concept. It speaks of our past deliverance from sin's penalty, our present progressive liberation from its power, and our future release from its presence. Salvation is a matter of personal trust in a living Savior, and this will be evidenced by open confession. Paul could not envision belief existing without a corresponding testimony. Confession verifies and confirms faith, and the person who truly believes on Christ will make it known.

C. *The Old Restrictions Rescinded*

The salvation which believers enjoy under grace is not only more complete and more easily comprehended than that under law, but also more readily accessible to all without distinction. Under law, Gentiles could be saved only by becoming proselytes to the Hebrew faith, and even then could not share all its privileges. A sharp line of demarcation between Jew and Gentile was maintained. New Testament salvation, however, eliminates all such distinctions. It is addressed to "whosoever," and no race or class of persons has any claim of priority or privilege over others. Therefore Paul declares,

> For the scripture saith, Whosoever believeth on him shall not be ashamed.
> For there is no difference between the Jew and the Greek; for the same Lord over all is rich unto all that call upon him.
> For whosoever shall call upon the name of the Lord shall be saved (Rom. 10:11-13).

Quoting from the Old Testament to show that God was concerned for the salvation of all, even under the dispensation of law, the apostle asserts that the Lord Jesus is eager to display His riches and generosity to *all* who call upon Him.

The words, "whosoever shall call upon the name of the Lord," are a quotation from Joel 2:32, which speaks of invoking the name of "Jehovah." Paul, using the name "Lord," his favorite designation for Jesus Christ, indicates that Christ is God, and extends an invitation to all. If you are conscious of your deep guilt before God and earnestly desire forgiveness and victory over sin, you are directed to call upon Jesus Christ, believe He died for your sins and was resurrected from the power of death. He will hear your cry and will bestow upon you all the blessings of salvation. You will then be constrained to tell others the good news. God's gracious invitation is extended to "whosoever." This includes you!

17

Judgment and Grace

The history of the Jewish nation since the time of Christ has been marked by one dire catastrophe after another. In A.D. 70, the city of Jerusalem was destroyed by Titus the Roman general, when more than one million of its citizens were slaughtered. Sixty-five years later the Jewish National State collapsed, some 500,000 were killed, and all Jews were expulsed from Judea and Jerusalem. During the following centuries hundreds and thousands of them have been executed or expelled from the lands in which they lived. In our own century Hitler and his henchmen ruthlessly killed nearly six million of them. Yet in 1948, over 1800 years after the complete disruption of the Jewish state, Israel once again became a recognized nation. Moreover, Jewish population today is well over twelve million, and about three million are living in Palestine. The preservation of Israel is a miracle. When Frederick the Great asked his chaplain to give him in a word the strongest evidence for the Christian faith, the reply was, "The Jew, Sir!" No other nation on earth has given such evidence of indestructibility.

Is Israel's national existence today merely an amazing phenomenon without great significance? Or has God preserved this people to fulfill an important role in His program for the future? The answer to these questions is given in Romans 11.

I. Israel's "Fall" and "Fullness"

The apostle begins his discussion of Israel's spiritual blindness by asking a question he knows his opponents will raise.

> I say, then, Hath God cast away his people? . . . (Rom. 11:1).

The Jews had been accustomed to a special relationship to God, and undoubtedly were both offended and confused by Paul's plain statement in Romans 10:12 that in the Church no distinction between Jew and Gentile existed.

A. *Israel's Fall*

The apostle unequivocally declares that Israel's fall is temporary, judicial, and purposeful, as he appeals to his own ancestry to explain the vehemence of his statement.

1. Temporary

The question "Hath God cast away his people?" is answered by a vigorous, NO! Paul declares,

> . . . God forbid. . . .
> God hath not cast away his people whom he foreknew . . .
> (Rom. 11:1, 2).

That Israel's present state is only temporary is reiterated in verse 11. Even as a man who stumbles may recover himself, so Israel has stumbled but not to a complete and irrevocable fall.

> I say, then, Have they stumbled that they should fall? God forbid . . . (Rom. 11:11).

In addition to this straightforward declaration that his nation has not been totally and finally rejected by God, the apostle sets forth evidence for his assertion. Reviewing Israel's history, he points out that there has always been a believing remnant. He reminds his readers that even during the dark days of Elijah seven thousand people did not succumb to idolatry, and says that a similar remnant exists in his own time.

> . . . Know ye not what the scripture saith of Elijah? how he maketh intercession to God against Israel, saying,
> Lord, they have killed thy prophets, and dug down thine altars; and I am left alone, and they seek my life.
> But what saith the answer of God unto him? I have reserved to myself seven thousand men who have not bowed the knee to the image of Baal.
> Even so, then, at this present time also there is a remnant according to the election of grace (Rom. 11:2-5).

This divine preservation of a remnant is not only proof that the setting aside of Israel is temporary, it is also a manifestation of God's grace. He mercifully spared the whole nation because a small minority remained true to Him, and even the majority did not taste the wrath that rightfully could have been poured on them. Furthermore, even the genuine believers in Israel were the recipients of grace, for they in no sense earned or merited favor with God.

> And if by grace, then is it no more of works; otherwise grace is no more grace . . . (Rom. 11:6).

The apostle therefore makes crystal-clear his deep conviction that God has not permanently cast off His people. He knows this by direct revelation, and he also sees in the believing remnant, which the Lord has graciously preserved, an outward token of God's intention to restore the nation to favor and fellowship.

2. Judicial

Although Israel's fall is temporary, it is nevertheless an act of judgment on the part of God. The unbelieving majority has been made morally and spiritually insensitive.

> What then? Israel hath not obtained that which he seeketh for; but the election hath obtained it, and the rest were blinded
>
> (According as it is written, God hath given them the spirit of slumber, eyes that they should not see, and ears that they should not hear) unto this day (Rom. 11:7, 8).

The verb in verse 7, which the authorized version translates "blinded," is *poroun,* and the noun form of this word is a medical term meaning "a callous." It is used to describe the hard formation around a bone when a fracture is mending, or the toughened layers of skin on the hand of one who habitually uses a tool like a hoe or shovel. In the moral and spiritual realm, callouses are formed on the souls of people when they deliberately ignore God's truth, or live in willful wickedness. This is what Israel had done, and now God in judgment had "given them the spirit of slumber." The word translated "slumber" is *katanuxis,* which literally means a "pricking" or "stinging," and came to be used to describe the numbness which results from the sting of certain insects. God in judgment sent a "numbness of spirit" upon those who had defiantly hardened themselves against the truth, and whose ears were deafened to His further appeals.

By way of application, let me issue a solemn warning to every person who is rejecting Christ or living immorally against better knowledge. If you continue on this course you will become increasingly insensitive to the horror of sin, and will finally become completely unresponsive to God's voice.

3. Purposeful

Israel's temporary fall, while an act of God's judgment, has behind it a loving design. By allowing His chosen nation to trip, God made possible the working out of His beneficent purposes for all mankind.

> I say, then, Have they stumbled that they should fall? God forbid; but rather through their fall salvation is come unto the Gentiles, to provoke them to jealousy (Rom. 11:11).

In the phrase "through their fall salvation is come unto the Gentiles," the word "fall" is the translation of the Greek term *paraptōma,* which means "a false step," or "transgression." The apostle thus continues the metaphor of the word "stumble," declaring that God permitted Israel to take this "false step" so that the Gospel could go directly to the Gentiles. Jewish unbelief became the occasion for Gentiles who receive Christ to become the spiritual equals with believing Jews. If the people of Israel had accepted their Messiah, they would have had the privilege of making Him known to the Gentiles. The chosen nation, however, stumbled at Christ, thus opening the door for Gentile co-equality with them in the Church.

When God ended the spiritual distinction between Jew and Gentile, He also had a loving purpose for the Israelites themselves. The Lord foresaw that some Israelites, witnessing the joyous and full salvation of believing Gentiles, would desire the same spiritual satisfaction, and turn to their Messiah.

To become interested in the Christian faith because of the fruit one observes in the lives of believers is not an unworthy motive. In fact, believers should live in such a manner that unsaved people will realize that faith in Christ is indeed the way of true peace and joy. If Christians would exhibit more fully the transforming power of the indwelling Holy Spirit, the Church of Jesus Christ would make a far greater impact than it does today. Not only Jews, but Gentiles as well, are looking for reality. They will listen only if they can see evidence of Christ's power in the lives of those who profess to know the Lord.

B. *Israel's Fullness*

Now shifting his emphasis from Israel's stumbling to her restoration, the apostle argues that if Israel's transgression in rejecting Christ brought blessing to the Gentiles, how much greater will be the worldwide benefit of Israel's return to God in faith.

> Now if the fall of them be the riches of the world, and the diminishing of them the riches of the Gentiles, how much more their fullness?
>
> For I speak to you Gentiles, inasmuch as I am the apostle of the Gentiles, I magnify mine office,
>
> If by any means I may provoke to jealousy them who are my flesh, and might save some of them (Rom. 11:12-14).

Addressing the non-Jewish believers, Paul declares that he, as "the apostle of the Gentiles," has been working diligently to reach them with the Gospel, and thereby has been promoting the spiritual welfare of individual Israelites. The more successful he was in reaching Gentiles for Christ, the greater the likelihood that some of his own people would desire to share in the blessings of salvation.

Turning again to the argument introduced in verse 12 the apostle declares,

> For if the casting away of them be the reconciling of the world, what shall the receiving of them be, but life from the dead? (Rom. 11:15).

When the nation of Israel accepts Christ as Messiah and Savior, it will be restored to the place of favor with God. Paul speaks of this event as "life from the dead." Some Bible teachers believe that in these words he refers to the physical resurrection of all Israel at the beginning of the millennial age. Others take this expression to mean that the nation, which has been dead in the sin of unbelief, will receive spiritual life. Both ideas are possible because the resurrection of Old Testament saints will take place at the beginning of the millennium, and also because a vast majority of Israelites living on earth at that time will be saved, spiritually passing from death to life. Furthermore, the entire earth will undergo a transformation which will be like "life from the dead." It will be marked by universal peace, prosperity, and justice. Isaiah declared that "the earth shall be full of the knowledge of the Lord, as the waters cover the sea" (Isa. 11:9). Yes, the small nation called Israel, struggling for survival in the Middle

East, is destined for spiritual renewal and restoration to God. When this takes place, the whole earth will experience unimaginable blessing.

II. ISRAEL'S REJECTION AND REINSTATEMENT

Still addressing Gentile believers, the apostle uses two metaphors to show that Israel can never be totally and finally rejected.

> For if the first fruit be holy, the lump is also holy; and if the root be holy, so are the branches (Rom. 11:16).

Under the law the Israelites offered the first portion of the dough or the first cake to God, and this act of consecration dedicated the entire batch. The metaphor of the root and branches expresses the same thought, and teaches that the nation of Israel is a cultivated olive tree, that its *root* is Abraham, and that individual Israelites make up the *branches.* Israel, rooted in the covenant promises made to Abraham, had been set apart for God and thus belonged to Him in a special manner. In that sense it was a holy nation.

A. *A Word of Warning to Gentiles*

The apostle introduces a second olive tree — a wild one — to develop his illustration, and to issue a warning to Gentile believers. He says that branches from the cultivated olive tree were cut off, and that branches from the wild tree were grafted in to replace them. (This was not a common practice in horticulture, but authorities like Sir William Ramsay point out that this was sometimes done to reinvigorate an olive tree that was not bearing much fruit.)

> And if some of the branches be broken off, and thou, being a wild olive tree, wert grafted in among them, and with them partakest of the root and fatness of the olive tree,
>
> Boast not against the branches. But if thou boast, thou bearest not the root, but the root thee.
>
> Thou wilt say, then, The branches were broken off, that I might be grafted in.
>
> Well; because of unbelief they were broken off, and thou standest by faith. Be not highminded, but fear;
>
> For if God spared not the natural branches, take heed lest he also spare not thee.
>
> Behold, therefore, the goodness and severity of God: on

> them who fell, severity; but toward thee, goodness, if thou
> continue in his goodness; otherwise thou also shalt be cut off
> (Rom. 11:17-22).

To understand this metaphor we must remember that not every
individual Israelite was a true believer, and therefore not a recipient of the full spiritual blessings of the covenant. The nation as
a whole never completely obeyed God, and therefore did not enjoy the entire scope of the physical and material promises. Furthermore, when Christ came as their Messiah, He was rejected
and crucified. Even after His resurrection the apostolic witness
was not received. God therefore brought about a change in His
program. Israel as a nation was temporarily set aside, and all unbelieving Jews lost their status as members of the covenant community. They are therefore pictured as being cut off, and re-
placed by Gentile believers in Christ. The tree inheriting the
spiritual aspects of the covenant which God made with Abraham
now became predominantly Gentile.

Paul proceeds to issue a warning against pride and complacency. Those who are only outwardly Christian, not possessing
genuine faith, will be dealt with exactly like the unbelieving Jews.
They will be cut off, and will not inherit eternal glory. If God removed the physical descendants of Abraham from the place of
blessing and privilege because of unbelief, He certainly will do
the same with those who are not the natural posterity of the patriarchs, if they are mere pretenders.

B. *The Word of Hope for Israel*

Having warned the Gentiles, Paul develops his illustration from
the field of horticulture to extend a promise to Israel. He declares that God is able to restore the nation to its former place of
priority when it is cured of unbelief.

> And they also, if they abide not still in unbelief, shall be
> grafted in; for God is able to graft them in again.
> For if thou wert cut out of the olive tree which is wild by
> nature, and wert grafted contrary to nature into a good olive
> tree, how much more shall these, who are the natural branches,
> be grafted into their own olive tree? (Rom. 11:23, 24).

Israel is an example of God's justice, truthfulness, and grace.
Therefore, when the nation was willfully disobedient and unbelieving, He sent catastrophic visitations of wrath. However, because God is always truthful, He will never break His promises.

Therefore, He has not abandoned or utterly repudiated the nation. The unbelief of Israel will someday be changed into faith, and the nation will once again be the center of the divine program for the earth. It will be a testimonial to God's amazing grace.

These principles of judgment and mercy as exemplified in Israel's history have universal application. Because God always responds to sin and unbelief, the child of God who falls into sinful practices will experience chastening. God's Word declares,

> For whom the Lord loveth he chasteneth, and scourgeth every son whom he receiveth (Heb. 12:6).

If you have been born into God's family, the punishment for your sins has already been placed upon Jesus Christ. However, since God cannot tolerate continued disobedience in the lives of His children, He chastens believers, displaying both His holy aversion to sin and His gracious concern for their ultimate welfare.

Unsaved friend, you also must reckon with God's justice and grace. If you have never truly received Christ, remember that though God is patient His justice will inevitably be displayed. He is merciful, and may postpone judgment, but do not mistake God's delays as indications that you are immune from punishment. Every sin will eventually be given a just recompense. God has mingled long-suffering and patience with His justice to give you an opportunity to repent and believe on Christ. We urge you therefore to receive Jesus Christ as your Lord and Savior today.

18

The God of History

Many people, sensitive to the agony of the ages, the heartbreak of history, and the injustice and pain of the present, have found it difficult to believe that a holy and loving God rules the universe. They have a tendency to deny the supernatural altogether, or to believe in some kind of impersonal power that is neither omniscient, omnipresent, holy, nor loving. Christians, however, are deeply convinced that the Creator and Sustainer of the universe is indeed a personal Being who hates sin, loves mankind, and is in ultimate control of all things. They also know that men and women, as free moral agents responsible to God, are guilty of breaking His holy laws, and that this is the reason sorrow, suffering, and injustice are present in the world. Though believers in Christ cannot satisfactorily explain every detail of divine providence, they are certain that God is directing history to a glorious eternal consummation. They know also that He will be glorified and universally vindicated when every created being acknowledges the lordship of Jesus Christ. Paul declares that,

> . . . at the name of Jesus every knee should bow, of things in heaven, and things in earth, and things under the earth,
> And that every tongue should confess that Jesus Christ is Lord, to the glory of God, the Father (Phil. 2:10, 11).

However, before the dawning of eternity in the new heaven and new earth, God will bring human history to a climax in a thousand-year period during which wars, social injustice, poverty and disease will no longer plague mankind. Jeremiah spoke of this era when he said,

> Behold, the days come, saith the LORD, that I will raise unto David a righteous Branch, and a King shall reign and prosper, and shall execute justice and righteousness in the earth.
> In his days Judah shall be saved, and Israel shall dwell safely;

and this is his name whereby he shall be called, THE LORD OUR RIGHTEOUSNESS (Jer. 23:5, 6).

In Romans 11:25-32, the apostle Paul sets forth the great truth that these plans and purposes will not be frustrated by human sin and unbelief. In fact, he points out that in infinite wisdom the Lord not only permitted sin to invade the world He had made, but that He uses even the disobedience of men to further His beneficent program.

I. GOD — HIS GRACIOUS OVERRULING OF HUMAN FAILURE

History, both Biblical and secular, does not present a flattering picture of the moral and spiritual quality of mankind. In every age men everywhere have rejected the truth, lived for self-gratification, and have set their wills against the Lord. This is true of both the Gentile world and the nation of Israel. Yet God will carry out His eternal purposes.

A. *Overcoming Gentile Ungodliness*

Pride is one of man's most grievous sins and an ever-present danger even for Christians. Knowing that Gentile believers might be tempted to look down upon the Jews, Paul declares a "mystery" — a truth they would not have understood except by revelation. God's purpose is that Israel's partial blindness will end when the "fullness" or "full complement" of the Gentiles has been brought into the Church.

> For I would not, brethren, that ye should be ignorant of this mystery, lest ye should be wise in your own conceits: that blindness in part is happened to Israel, until the fullness of the Gentiles be come in (Rom. 11:25).

God has been building His Church since the day of Pentecost, and has brought into it millions of non-Jewish people. He has done this in pure grace, and through the convicting and quickening work of the Holy Spirit in the hearts of sin-blinded and depraved people, without which none would be saved. However, the Gentile world in general has rejected the Gospel, thus continuing to demonstrate man's utter perverseness and depravity.

During the period from Adam to Noah, knowledge of God was transmitted from generation to generation, and men also knew that God was to be approached through sacrifice. The Lord tested mankind in an atmosphere of freedom from outward restraint, but the human race became so wicked that all but one family had to be destroyed in the Flood.

God then established human government as a check upon man's evil tendencies, but again his perversity was displayed. Tyrants like Nimrod (Gen. 10:6-12) began to oppress others, and people degenerated into vile paganism. The heathen world out of which God called Abraham was marked by cruelty, oppression, sensual idolatry, and unspeakable lasciviousness. The human race thus demonstrated that it will not obey God, whether in the atmosphere of freedom or under delegated authority.

Turning from mankind in general, God then revealed Himself in a special way to Abraham. From him He brought into existence the nation of Israel that it might become the repository of His truth, and the channel through which the promised Messiah would come. After Christ's incarnation, death, and resurrection, the Gentile world was once again given a glorious opportunity because Israel had officially rejected the Savior. The Gospel was preached to all without distinction, Gentiles being offered equality with Jews in the Church. However, the vast majority of men still reject God, demonstrating the truth of Paul's words,

> . . . There is none righteous, no, not one;
> There is none that understandeth, there is none that seeketh after God.
> They are all gone out of the way, they are together become unprofitable; there is none that doeth good, no, not one (Rom. 3:10-12).

Yes, man has given ample proof that he is in continual rebellion against God. Fancying himself to be good, he likes to think in terms of earning his own salvation. He therefore resents the message of the Gospel which tells him that he is utterly depraved, and that he cannot be redeemed apart from the sacrificial death of Jesus Christ. God is constructing His Church, however, in spite of man's stubbornness, pride, and spiritual blindness. He is "visiting the Gentiles [nations], to take out of them a people for his name" (Acts 15:14). Someday, perhaps very soon, the fullness of the Gentiles will come in, and the Church will be "caught up" to reign with Christ.

B. *Overruling Israel's Unbelief*

God gave Israel the covenants, the law of Moses, the ritual of the Tabernacle and Temple, and the ministry of inspired prophets.

Yet the nation's history is marked by unbelief and disobedience. For example, after being delivered from slavery in Egypt, the people murmured against the Lord and disobeyed Him ten times during the period of desert wandering. As time went on, they repeatedly fell into the degrading worship of heathen idols, turned a deaf ear to the prophets, and finally refused their Messiah. Speaking to the leaders of Israel after the nation had rejected Jesus Christ, Stephen declared,

> Ye stiff-necked and uncircumcised in heart and ears, ye do always resist the Holy Spirit; as your fathers did, so do ye.
>
> Which of the prophets have not your fathers persecuted? And they have slain them who showed before of the coming of the Just One, of whom ye have been now the betrayers and murderers;
>
> Who have received the law by the disposition of angels, and have not kept it (Acts 7:51-53).

Though Israel's spiritual attitude to this day is characterized by unbelief and disobedience, the Bible declares that this state of spiritual blindness is neither total nor permanent. After the full complement of the Gentiles has been brought into the Church, God will once again deal with His chosen people and turn their unbelief to faith.

> And so all Israel shall be saved; as it is written, There shall come out of Zion the Deliverer, and shall turn away ungodliness from Jacob;
>
> For this is my covenant unto them, when I shall take away their sins (Rom. 11:26, 27).

The nation will pass through a period of great tribulation, and during this time of affliction Israel will repent and believe on Jesus Christ. Daniel spoke of this event when he said,

> And at that time shall Michael stand up, the great prince who standeth for the children of thy people, and there shall be a time of trouble, such as never was since there was a nation even to that same time; and at that time thy people shall be delivered, every one that shall be found written in the book (Dan. 12:1).

The prophet Zechariah also saw this day, and spoke touchingly of Israel's return to God,

> And it shall come to pass that in all the land, saith the LORD, two parts in it shall be cut off and die; but the third shall be left in it.
>
> And I will bring the third part through the fire, and will refine them as silver is refined, and will test them as gold is tested; they shall call on my name, and I will hear them. I will say, It is my people; and they shall say, The Lord is my God (Zech. 13:8, 9).

In the twenty-eighth and twenty-ninth verses of Romans 11, Paul proceeds to point out that Israel today is living in estrangement from God, and that Gentile believers are enjoying spiritual equality with believing Jews. However, the Lord elected this people to fulfill a special role upon the earth, and made definite promises to the patriarchs. God will never repent of the choice He has made of Israel, but will yet fulfill His vows toward them.

> As concerning the gospel, they are enemies for your sakes; but as touching the election, they are beloved for the fathers' sakes.
>
> For the gifts and calling of God are without repentance (Rom. 11:28, 29).

C. *Universal Blessing*

God's ultimate purpose in all His dealings is to show mercy upon Jew and Gentile alike. When God turned away from the nations in general, establishing a special covenant with Abraham and his descendants, His purpose was to bring salvation to all mankind through the Jews, not to consign the nations to eternal perdition. Israel had to be a distinct people, however, in order to preserve the line of Christ. Therefore, the Jews were given the land of Palestine, a territory hedged about by mountains, deserts, and water, without a natural port, and no river leading to its interior. The Jews nevertheless were still to be the Lord's witness to the nations. The fact that God desired His name to be known everywhere, even before the coming of Christ, is clearly expressed by Isaiah. He prophesied concerning Cyrus, a heathen king whom he declared God would use to help His chosen people. He said that God's reason for raising up Cyrus was,

> That they may know from the rising of the sun, and from the west, that there is none beside me. I am the LORD, and there is none else (Isa. 45:6).

The nation of Israel was strategically placed by God where it could be distinct, and yet fulfill its function as God's missionary nation. Therefore, Palestine is also "the center of the earth" (Ezek. 38:12), the place where three continents nearly touch, and the point at which the West and the East meet. The chosen people failed to carry out their task, however, because of unbelief and disobedience.

Paul reminds the Gentiles that their own unbelief had originally led God to single out Israel for special blessing, but now the disobedience of the Jews had returned the Lord's favor to the Gentiles. The apostle asserts that God will once again in the future have mercy on His ancient people. He sums it up by saying that both Jew and Gentile have been imprisoned in disobedience in order that the Lord might bestow His grace upon all.

> For as ye in times past have not believed God, yet have now obtained mercy through their unbelief,
> Even so have these also now not believed, that through your mercy they also may obtain mercy.
> For God hath concluded them all in unbelief, that he might have mercy upon all (Rom. 11:30-32).

God has thus demonstrated the total depravity of Jew and Gentile alike that all may feel their need of His undeserved favor. He is not declaring that every individual will be saved, for some like Pharaoh persistently refuse divine mercy. All do not receive salvation because many will not accept it, and thus exclude themselves. Nevertheless, God's offer of salvation remains the same. It is equally gracious and universal, whether men accept His mercy or not.

Friend, God loves you and is willing to show His grace in you. He has given you a dark picture of yourself as a totally depraved sinner, unable to earn favor with Him, that you might abandon all self-effort and believe on Jesus Christ. Whether you are a Jew or Gentile, a relatively moral person or a dissolute outcast from decent society, you need salvation through the Lord Jesus. Acknowledge your sinfulness and helplessness and trust Christ. Believe that He died for your sin, confess your need, and receive Him as your Savior.

II. GOD — HIS SUPREME EXCELLENCE AND GLORY

Paul now turns from argument and instruction to praise. The seeking of the mind is exchanged for the adoration of the heart! In this expression of devotion the apostle first ascribes praise to God because His being and ways are beyond all human comprehension; then he glorifies the Lord by declaring Him to be the Source, Support, and Goal of all things.

A. *God's Incomprehensible Being and Ways*

Overwhelmed as he contemplates the glories of salvation's plan, the apostle says,

> Oh, the depth of the riches both of the wisdom and knowledge of God! How unsearchable are his judgments, and his ways past finding out! (Rom. 11:33).

The riches of God's wisdom and knowledge are inexhaustible. The world presents a picture of chaos and turmoil, for on every hand there are conflicts between individuals and nations, races and religions. Injustice and immorality abound everywhere. Yet, ruling over all is a God of infinite holiness and love. He has the wisdom and knowledge to arrange and adapt all things to the fulfillment of His holy purpose in a manner transcending human thought and calling forth adoring praise. No finite creature is able fully to understand the decisions of the Almighty or trace the mysterious ways He carries out His purposes. Tersteegen said, "A God comprehended is no God at all." Recognizing this, the believer is content to reach out with his mind as far as he can; then, when the limit of his mental capacity is reached, to accept by faith the mysteries he cannot comprehend and to adore his Maker and Redeemer. In Romans 11:34 and 35, Paul quotes Old Testament Scriptures as he asks three rhetorical questions, all implying a negative answer.

> For who hath known the mind of the Lord? Or who hath been his counselor?
> Or who hath first given to him, and it shall be recompensed unto him again?

These words declare the Lord's complete independence and self-sufficiency. No creature in Heaven or earth can know the mind of God unless He chooses to reveal it. No created being gave advice in the determination of His eternal counsels. Furthermore, not one of His moral creatures has done anything for God which makes the Creator his debtor. God owes no one! Every blessing men receive proceeds only from His loving heart, and is a display of His mercy and grace.

B. *God's Infinite Glory*

In one mighty surge of devotion, Paul worships, saying,

> For of him, and through him, and to him, are all things: to whom be glory forever. Amen (Rom. 11:36).

In this grand yet brief benediction the apostle sums up his feelings as he closes the doctrinal portion of this epistle. What more can one say than this? All things come from God since He is the Creator. All things exist through Him, for He sustains them and directs them to their proper end. All things are to Him, for He is the One to whose glory they will issue. The triune God is the Alpha and Omega, the beginning and the end, the first and the last. All the outworkings of history will redound to His eternal glory, and every redeemed creature will forever ascribe praise to Him. In these closing words Paul already seems to have captured the spirit of that heavenly company described in Revelation as they sing, "Blessing, and honor, and glory, and power be unto him that sitteth upon the throne, and unto the Lamb forever and ever" (Rev. 5:13).

19

The Transformed Life

People who like to wrestle with theological and philosophical problems but do not practice godliness in their daily lives are a reproach to the cause of Christ. They certainly do not follow the apostle Paul's example. Though his great mind swept the heights and depths, he never lost himself in idle speculation. He reached out as far as the human intellect can, and then, accepting by faith that which he could not understand, he always came back to the practical matter of the believer's conduct. He never side-stepped God's moral demands upon his own life. Himself a radiant Christian, he was confident that by God's grace every believer could be victorious over doubt, despondency, and sin.

Therefore, having declared the great truths of salvation, having answered the objections of the critics, and having dealt with some of the great problems in the minds of sincere seekers for truth, Paul now sets forth practical guidelines for Christian living. In the first two verses of Romans 12, the scope of this lesson, the writer appeals for an act of commitment which will issue in a life of satisfaction and spiritual power. The basic elements of such a life are first presented, then the means by which it is maintained.

I. THE PRINCIPLES OF THE TRANSFORMED LIFE

The godly walk of a Christian originates in God's supernatural salvation, is motivated by gratitude, and is launched by an initial act of dedication.

A. *Its Source — Redemption*

Paul begins the twelfth chapter of Romans with the words, "I beseech you *therefore,*" pointing back not only to the climactic exclamation which closed the eleventh chapter, but to all the preceding truths expressed in the epistle. No person can obey the directives of Romans 12 unless he first realizes the significance of his union with Christ, the spring from which Christian victory flows. In Romans 5 the apostle had taught that the believer no longer stands in the place of condemnation, but enjoys favor with God. He is therefore able to rejoice in the midst of life's heavy pressures, knowing that suffering develops patience, and this in turn leads to a genuine experience of Christian love and hope (Rom. 5:1-5). In chapter 6 the believer's baptism is declared to be a picture of union with Christ, signifying death to the former state, and a walk in "newness of life" (Rom. 6:1-4). On the basis of this same oneness with Christ, Paul had instructed believers to consider themselves "to be dead indeed unto sin, but alive unto God" (Rom. 6:11). In the striking autobiographical seventh chapter, Paul had revealed the truth that no believer can overcome the power of indwelling sin in his own strength. Chapter 8 sets forth the riches, joy, and triumph of the child of God who lives under the control of the indwelling Holy Spirit.

Therefore, the fountainhead of the believer's strength to overcome indwelling sin lies in the gracious provisions of God. The Christian, possessing a vital union with Jesus Christ, and having been made the recipient of the indwelling Holy Spirit, is no longer bound by the shackles of sin, but is enabled to live on a spiritual plateau which the natural man can never reach.

B. *Its Stimulus — Gratitude*

The apostle urges believers to godly living by reminding them of the "mercies of God."

> I beseech you therefore, brethren, *by the mercies of God* . . . (Rom. 12:1).

If you are a Christian you should often reflect upon what the Lord in infinite compassion has done for you. He has pardoned your sins, removed you from your old standing as guilty and condemned, and made you His own dear child. Jesus Christ, your intercessor in Heaven, guarantees your complete salvation. The Holy Spirit within you enables you to defeat the power of indwelling sin, gives you the consciousness of divine sonship, and takes over for you when you do not know how to pray. You can therefore be certain that all things work together for your good, and that nothing can ever separate you from God's love. Furthermore, the Lord is directing history to a glorious consummation in which you will have a wonderful part. O the mercies of

God! How undeserving we are! Christian friend, meditate upon these great truths, and let your gratitude be the stimulus to a life of glad obedience and unselfish service.

C. *Its Sum and Substance — Dedication*

This transformed life is impossible, however, without absolute submission to God. It is initiated by an act of surrender, as the believer yields his body to the Lord. Paul says,

> I beseech you therefore, brethren, by the mercies of God, *that ye present your bodies a living sacrifice,* holy, acceptable unto God, which is your reasonable service (Rom. 12:1).

The Greek verb translated *"present"* is in the aorist tense, which indicates an act of dedication.

1. The Body

Specifically, the believer's body must be put at God's disposal. This demand is another indication of the wide difference between the Christian faith and the religions of men. The pagans considered the body to be merely a prison house, and looked upon death as good because it released the spirit from this vile corporeal existence. Most of the religionists of Paul's day, thinking all that mattered was the soul or spirit, engaged in degraded lustful practices without a feeling of remorse.

The Christian, however, recognizes that the body has been an integral part of man from the time of creation, that its dissolution comes because of sin, and that death is therefore abnormal. He also knows that God became incarnated in the person of Jesus Christ, revealing that the body in itself is not sinful. The Lord Jesus Christ is living in Heaven today in a glorified human body, and has assured believers that they too will someday be like Him. Furthermore, the believer's body in this present world has become the temple of the Holy Spirit, the instrument in which all human service is rendered to God. Therefore, instead of taking a low view of the physical self, the believer is to present his body once for all to God, indicating thereby that he will use it to serve the Lord. Every Christian must realize that he has a solemn responsibility to glorify God in his body.

2. A "Living Sacrifice"

The Word further specifies that the body be yielded to God as a "living sacrifice." The language Paul uses is that of the Old

Testament ritual. Yet there is a striking contrast between the slain offerings Israel brought to God and that which He asks of us. The human body is not presented for the purpose of being slain. On the contrary, a Christian is to think of himself as one formerly dead in trespasses and sins but now the possessor of eternal life, even though he lives in a body which must ultimately undergo physical death. He yields this body as the instrument through which he, as a redeemed human personality, can serve God. While the Old Testament believers in their sacrifices gave God something they possessed, the New Testament saint gives himself to God.

This living sacrifice to God is termed "holy, acceptable unto God." The believer, recognizing that his body belongs to the Lord, considers it set apart for God's service, and therefore does not use it for the gratification of sinful desires. Moral purity is an absolute requirement of God, and the person who indulges in licentious living cannot present his body "holy, acceptable to God." In this day of moral laxness, Christians need to be reminded that fornication, adultery, and every form of illicit sexual expression is evil in the sight of God. God demands chastity, and His grace will enable every believer to achieve a virtuous life.

3. Rational Service

Paul proceeds to declare that this dedication of our bodies as holy and acceptable unto God is our "reasonable service." Many translators render this phrase "spiritual service," and others "spiritual worship." The Greek word used here pertains to the reason or the mind, and therefore does not really mean "spiritual." It is better translated "reasonable" or "rational." Moreover, the Greek word rendered "service" does indeed convey the idea of worship — not the worship of the sanctuary, but of everyday life. The Christian is to engage in all his activities — whether in the factory, the office, the mine, or on the farm — in the spirit of conscious, intelligent, and consecrated worship. We are to yield our bodies to God so completely that we worship Him in whatever we do and wherever we are. This does not mean that we offer formal prayers or quote Scripture verses all the time, but that we are ever to be conscious of God, honoring Him in all things. The ordinary duties of life become acts of worship for one who has surrendered his body to God.

In summary, the transformed life begins with an act of dedication, involving the surrender of the body to God. This means that the believer will not seek to fulfill fleshly lusts, but rather will hold his body in high esteem as God's temple, keeping it morally pure, and utilizing it as a vehicle of loving service to God.

II. THE CONTINUANCE OF THE TRANSFORMED LIFE

This surrender of one's body to God has additional implications for the believer, as taught in Romans 12:2. Such a life precludes conformity to the world, requires transformation, and issues in spiritual enlightenment.

> And be not conformed to this world, but be ye transformed by the renewing of your mind, that ye may prove what is that good, and acceptable, and perfect, will of God (Rom. 12:2).

A. *Its Prohibition — Conformity*

The injunction "be not conformed to this world" is sometimes criticized because it is negative in nature, but such an objection has absolutely no validity. The prohibitions of the Bible are necessary because of sin. Eight of the Ten Commandments are negative in nature, and the whole New Testament affirms the truth that turning to Christ involves renunciation of evil. Therefore, a consecrated believer is to reject the external and fleeting fashion of this world.

The word translated "world" is often rendered "age," and refers to the present order which Paul terms "evil" in Galatians 1:4, and of which he declares that Satan is its "god" in II Corinthians 4:4. The apostle John, speaking of this same world system, says, "The whole world lieth in wickedness" (I John 5:19). This satanically dominated age is an enemy to the believer, and must be recognized as such.

The term "conformed" is derived from the noun *skēma*, and refers to the outward form of a person or thing — that which may vary from year to year, or even from day to day. To be conformed to this age means to allow the changing and external fashion of this world to mold one's thoughts and actions. Mankind in general thinks only in terms of this temporal and transitory age. The believer, however, is not to allow himself to be wrapped up in the plans and ambitions which have only this life in view. He is to resist the efforts of this evil system to squeeze him into its mold. He must look always at life with eternal values in mind, and govern himself by the changeless principles of God's holy Word.

B. *Its Prescription — Transformation*

Turning from the negative to the positive, Paul moves on to say, "But be ye transformed by the renewing of your mind." We must undergo a continual inner change. The verb here rendered "transformed" is used by Matthew and Mark to describe the transfiguration of Jesus Christ. Our English term "metamorphosis" comes from this word. The root is *morphē,* which means the essential unchanging shape or element of anything. For example, the *skēma* or outward form of a man is different when he is working in his garden than when he is dressed to attend a wedding. However, his *morphē,* or "inner self," is the same. The change in the life of the believer issues from within. The moment a person accepts Jesus Christ he receives a new life from God called the "new birth" or "regeneration." This newly imparted life gradually influences every aspect of the human personality. The Bible calls this process "sanctification," and Paul says it takes place through "the renewing of the mind." God gives those who are His own the faculty of correct spiritual vision, while the person who rejects God becomes the victim of an increasingly distorted view of moral and spiritual values. The believer, who sees things properly, grows more holy, whereas those who turn away from the truth become increasingly depraved in their conduct. The Holy Spirit, you see, works in the believer's center of consciousness, bringing about a gradual change in his life. The Christian who has yielded his body to God and consistently rejects the influences of this evil world will become more Christlike day by day, as Paul declares in II Corinthians 3:18,

> But we all, with unveiled face beholding as in a mirror the glory of the Lord, are changed into the same image from glory to glory, even as by the Spirit of the Lord.

C. *Its Product — Enlightenment*

The believer who is being transformed by the inner working of the Holy Spirit will enjoy a wonderful life of true spiritual realization. Paul says,

> . . . that ye may prove what is that good, and acceptable, and perfect, will of God (Rom. 12:2).

The word translated "prove" means "to appreciate," or "to learn by experience."

This "will of God" does not refer to God's secret decrees covering the hidden and future details of our earthly lives, but to his *revealed* will. The believer, having obeyed the command of Romans 12:1, does not permit himself to be molded by the fashions of this world, but knows the inner renewing work of the Holy Spirit, and will learn by experience that God's commandments and regulations are *good,* for they promote his welfare. He also learns that the will of God is "acceptable." This means that he will rejoice to know that God is pleased with him. Even as a child beams with happiness when parents express their approval, so the believer finds great joy in the assurance that God looks upon him with delight. Furthermore, the will of God is also *perfect,* and the obedient believer enjoys true satisfaction. An unsaved psychologist recently admitted that one of the great problems he encounters in his clients is a feeling of utter futility, emptiness, and aimlessness. Men need to feel somehow that life has a purpose, and that they are, at least to some extent, reaching that goal. The believer in Christ has the satisfaction of knowing that he is progressing in that for which God made him. He knows that he will not reach complete perfection here, but is assured that it will be his someday in Heaven.

In conclusion, the Christian learns by experience that the will of God is good, rewarding, and satisfying. The believer who finds life stagnant, fruitless, and lacking in true spiritual contentment, has not presented his body to God, and he is either conforming to the fashions of this world or failing to walk in obedience to the revealed will of God. Such a person is cheating himself of the spiritual richness and fullness God would have him enjoy.

Friend, in an act of dedication, today present your body as a living sacrifice to God. Do not allow this evil world system to shape your way of life, but submit yourself to the gracious working of the indwelling Holy Spirit. You will never be sorry for this decision.

20

The Christian Life in Action

The spiritual state of the average church today is deplorable. Many believers are extremely lax in their devotional life; they seldom witness, set too much value upon this world's pleasures and possessions, and do not have a strong yearning for Christlikeness. Furthermore, petty envyings and strife among the saints often disillusion new Christians, thereby rendering ineffective the witness of the church in the community. No wonder God's people are not making a greater impact upon the world!

Believers need to consider seriously the message of Romans 12. It establishes principles which regulate the believer's service in the church and govern his conduct in the ordinary course of life. No believer is truly honoring God unless he lives out these practical directives in day-by-day consistent behavior.

I. IN CHRISTIAN SERVICE

The local church plays a vital role in God's program for this age. From the beginning of the apostolic ministry, the believers banded together for fellowship, for edification, and for Christian service. Most of Paul's epistles were written to local assemblies, and God equipped men to fill specific offices — apostles, prophets, evangelists, pastors and teachers (Eph. 4:11); bishops and deacons (I Tim. 3).

In addition, the Lord also distributed various graces and abilities. Some of these "grace gifts" were temporary, serving only during the apostolic period, while others are still with us today. In Romans 12 the apostle deals with these "grace gifts," and likens the Church to the human body, thus illustrating both the oneness of believers and the responsibility of each Christian to fulfill the task God has assigned him. Concerned that Christians have a proper attitude before engaging in their service for God,

Paul declares that it must be preceded by spiritual preparation
He then enumerates the different gifts possessed by believers.

A. *Spiritual Preparation*

God has brought people into the Church from the most diverse
backgrounds, and with vastly differing temperaments and capacities. Some possess more inherent ability than others, and have
also received greater spiritual gifts from God. They are able to
exercise more leadership and will undoubtedly receive greater
human adulation. The believer must therefore be spiritually prepared so that he will not resent those who have greater gifts,
nor despise those less gifted.

1. Sober Self-evaluation

The yielded believer will neither refuse a humble position because of envy or pride, nor reject a place of responsibility due to
false humility. Paul says,

> For I say, through the grace given unto me, to every man
> that is among you, not to think of himself more highly than
> he ought to think, but to think soberly, according as God hath
> dealt to every man the measure of faith (Rom. 12:3).

Every Christian should assess his own capabilities without con-
ceit or false modesty. God has given individuals varying natural
capacities, and has also bestowed "a measure of faith" upon each
person. The faith of which Paul speaks here is not "saving faith,"
but an "achieving faith," a "working-for-God faith." (Paul himself never forgot that God had given him the "grace of apostleship," an honor of which he felt completely unworthy.) Every
believer receives a "measure of faith" corresponding to the task
God gives him to accomplish. For this reason every Christian
must humbly recognize that whatever his native ability or spiritual gifts, they are his by the grace of God. This will help him to
be grateful to the Lord, to be humble in his attitude toward
those who have less than he, and avoid envying those with
greater capacities and gifts. Christian friend, are you thankful
and modest as you reflect upon what God has graciously given
you? Or are you resentful, envious, and unfaithful — a hindrance to the cause of Christ? Contemplate what God has done
for you and give Him thanks.

2. Sincere Self-Abnegation

Having urged believers to carefully evaluate their gifts and abilities, Paul proceeds to emphasize that every Christian must seek the welfare of all his fellow-believers rather than his own selfish interests. Using the human body as an illustration of the corporate life of believers, he points out that as each part of a person's body has a specific function, so individual Christians have essential roles to fulfill in the Church. Therefore, every believer, losing sight of personal honor, is to fill his particular niche, having in view the welfare of all the members of Christ. The apostle says,

> For as we have many members in one body, and all members have not the same office,
> So we, being many, are one body in Christ, and every one members one of another (Rom. 12:4, 5).

B. *Faithful Performance*

Not only must believers soberly evaluate their gifts and abilities, and sincerely renounce all selfishness, they also are responsible to be faithful in service. The apostle lists a number of the gifts God has given, and exhorts each Christian to exercise his particular gift to the best of his ability.

> Having then gifts differing according to the grace that is given to us, whether prophecy, let us prophesy according to the proportion of faith;
> Or ministry, let us wait on our ministering; or he that teacheth, on teaching;
> Or he that exhorteth, on exhortation; he that giveth, let him do it with liberality; he that ruleth, with diligence; he that showeth mercy, with cheerfulness (Rom. 12:6-8).

1. Prophecy

"Prophecy" is the inspired utterance of truth, and this gift does not exist today in the same form as during the apostolic era. The inerrant New Testament Scriptures are now in our hands, and the person who preaches Bible truths today, though not speaking by inspiration, in a real sense exercises the prophetic ministry. He is handling inspired truth, and what he says is God's Word to the extent that he truly declares what the Bible teaches.

This service for God is to be rendered "according to the proportion of faith." This means that the prophet of apostolic times was faithfully to declare the revelation God had given him, neither adding nor withholding anything. By the same token, the preacher today must be careful that he teaches as authoritative truth only what is clearly expressed in God's Word. Furthermore, he must be careful also not to withhold the proclamation of doctrines that are somewhat distasteful to him. To declare God's Word, whether in the inspired utterance of prophecy or in preaching, is indeed a solemn responsibility.

2. Ministering

The second gift, called "ministering" in the King James Version, refers perhaps to the work of deacons. The Greek word *diakonia* may be rendered "service," but is also used to specify the office of a deacon. The person called to this task must show genuine concern for the spiritual and physical well-being of fellow believers.

3. Teaching and Exhortation

The next gifts mentioned by Paul are "teaching and exhortation." Admonishing those who are called to teach and to exhort, he says that they must faithfully fulfill their respective callings. Bible scholars are not agreed regarding the distinctions between these two offices. Many believe that the *teacher* explained the Old Testament Scriptures and the new truths proclaimed by the prophets of the Early Church, while the *exhorter* sought to impress these teachings upon the heart, the conscience, and the will. Other Bible students consider the ministry of teaching as directed to the whole man — his intellect, his emotions, and his will — and hold that the gift of exhortation refers specifically to the ministry of comfort for those in affliction, sorrow, or pain. In the Church today some of God's servants possess the aptitude to explain Bible truths in simple and understandable language, while others have an ability to minister comfort in an unusual manner. As in the apostolic era, so in the present day, these two gifts are often exercised by the same person. In any case, God requires diligence and faithfulness.

4. Giving

Paul then names the grace of "giving." He declares that those who give are to do so with "simplicity," a term which connotes the idea of simple kindliness. A Christian should find delight in the sheer pleasure of giving and sharing. Undoubtedly, those who are blessed with material wealth are able to exercise this gift in greater measure than those who have less of this world's goods. Every Christian, however, can have a share in this wonderful privilege. He must never give to obtain influence and advantage for himself, nor because it will make him an object of praise, but always as a grateful expression of his love for God and his fellow men.

5. Leadership

The apostle continues by declaring that spiritual "leaders" are to rule "with diligence." They are to observe constant vigilance, for they are looked upon by God as shepherds of His flock (Acts 20:28), and are to watch for the souls of those under their care (Heb. 13:17). Peter says that men who exercise authority must do so with gladness, and are not to be motivated by greed or a desire for power (I Pet. 5:1-3). Leadership is a marvelous gift, but it also carries with it great responsibility, for Hebrews 13:17 declares that service is rendered with an awareness that they "must give account" to God.

6. Showing Mercy

The last gift mentioned, the faculty of "showing mercy," should be practiced by every Christian. Paul states that it is to be done "with cheerfulness," not with a grudging spirit or unhappy face. The Christian who finds delight in coming to the aid of one who is in difficulty renders a service that has value beyond measure. Another way of "showing mercy" is in forgiving those who have wronged us. Forgiveness must not be accompanied by an attitude of contempt, but must demonstrate a glad willingness to show mercy in a Christlike spirit.

Christian friend, what about your service to God in the Church? Have you soberly analyzed the gifts and abilities God has bestowed, and are you exercising them to the best of your ability? Or are you a lazy Christian who makes no effort to develop and utilize the gifts and capacities God has graciously given? Worse still, does a spirit of envy possess your heart so that you are somewhat rebellious against God and resentful toward those possessing greater gifts than yours? Remember, the pathway of blessing is that of grateful obedience and faithful service.

II. IN EVERYDAY LIVING

Paul, having instructed and admonished believers regarding their life within the Church, now establishes principles for ordinary, everyday living. His exhortations in Romans 12:9-13 may be classified as the practical expression of Christian love and hope.

A. *Christian Love in Action*

Every believer should always bear in mind the fact that apart from the substitutionary suffering and death of the Lord Jesus he would still be in his sins. Therefore, his conduct should be dictated by the love of Christ; that is, primarily by the Lord's love for him which precedes and motivates his own love for Christ. His devotion to the Savior is inevitably involved, however, and it deepens as he increasingly apprehends the greatness of Christ's love for him. Paul declares that this love expresses itself in a life of sincerity, affection, zeal, and generosity.

1. Sincerity

Christian love is marked first of all by sincerity. Paul says,

> Let love be without hypocrisy. Abhor that which is evil; cling to that which is good (Rom. 12:9).

No vice is more reprehensible than hypocrisy. To make an outward show of love, while in reality possessing ill will and hatred, is to imitate Judas Iscariot. No believer should make a pretense of love in order to gain his own selfish ends, nor is he to secretly admire evil while putting on a show of love for goodness. The person motivated by the love of Christ is sincere, hating evil and loving righteousness.

2. Affection

Paul proceeds to set forth a second mark of Christian love; namely, that of an affectionate regard for others.

> Be kindly affectioned one to another with brotherly love, in honor preferring one another (Rom. 12:10).

This exhortation has primary reference to the relationship of believers to one another. The Greek term *philostorgoi* (kindly affectioned) denotes the feeling that should exist between members of a family, and the Greek word translated "brotherly love" strengthens this concept. Believers are to have a strong natural affection for one another, marked by warmth, spontaneity, fidelity, and selflessness. As Christian parents are happy to stand aside when a son or daughter is honored, so believers should find keen delight whenever another child of God is exalted. The same spirit should manifest itself in the Christian's relationship to those outside of Christ. If this exhortation were taken seriously and practiced, what an impact would be made upon the community!

3. Zeal

The person whose life is impelled by the love of Christ will also be zealous in the performance of his Christian duties.

> Not slothful in business; fervent in spirit; serving the Lord (Rom. 12:11).

The phrase "not slothful in business" literally means, "not declining in zeal." He is to be "aglow with the Spirit" and to serve the Lord with enthusiasm and fervency.

4. Generosity

In addition, the consciousness of Christ's love will produce an openhearted spirit and a willingness to share.

> Distributing to the necessity of saints; given to hospitality (Rom. 12:13).

Every believer is to identify himself with the needs of other Christians, and to make them his own. He will therefore manifest true hospitality. The conditions brought on by persecution caused the early Christians to share their goods and to open their homes to one another. Though the situation is quite different today, the same spirit of sharing should still mark believers.

B. *Christian Hope in Action*

Paul continues his inspired directives by centering upon Christian hope — faith looking forward to the future. A recent study of patients in a large university hospital reported that hope is a real source of strength to dying people. However, this hope was that of a flickering belief that perhaps doctors would suddenly find a cure for the terminal illness. The horizon of hope in the thinking of an unsaved person is bounded by that which can be seen. The hope of the believer, on the other hand, looks to eternity with confidence. It is not a mere wish, but is based upon all that Jesus Christ has done, is doing, and has promised; it is grounded in the great redemptive facts recorded in the Bible. Christians look forward to Heaven, enjoying the prospect of an eternity without sin, pain, tears, or death, and therefore are able to manifest gladness, patience, and prayerfulness.

1. Gladness

The hope of the Christian is the source of true joy.

Rejoicing in hope . . . (Rom. 12:12).

No matter how grievous the affliction, the believer's hope enables him to rejoice. Even when believers sorrow — weeping because loved ones have died — their tears are different from those shed by the unsaved. Yes, believers do weep, they do experience sorrow, but not "as others who have no hope" (I Thess. 4:13). How wonderful the anticipation of reunion and glory!

2. Patience

This joy of hope makes the Christian steadfast in tribulation. Paul says,

. . . patient in tribulation . . . (Rom. 12:12).

Believers know that affliction and trials are part and parcel of life upon earth, and that they in a special way are called upon to suffer for Christ's sake. However, they are also assured that God is working all things for their good, that nothing can separate them from His love, and that eternal glory awaits them. This enables them to display patience, even in times of great difficulty.

3. Prayerfulness

Finally, the hope-filled believer relies upon communion with God.

. . . continuing diligently in prayer (Rom. 12:12).

Through prayer we receive the daily supply of grace needed to meet every crisis of life. The forward look of faith is made real

when we pray, and the temptation to discouragement is overcome through the response of God.

Christian friend, is the love of Christ a constraining and com-
pelling force in your life? Is it moving you to sincerity, affection, zeal, and generous love? What about hope? Do you look
forward with genuine anticipation to the day when you shall be
with Christ? Is your life marked by joy, steadfastness, and genuine piety? Read again these verses from Romans 12. Take them
seriously, asking the Holy Spirit to indelibly imprint them upon
your consciousness.

21

The Christian's Relationships

The inability of humans to get along with one another is apparent both on the international and domestic scenes. Lawsuits and divorce proceedings by the thousands are on the daily agenda of our courts. Riots and strikes make headlines almost every day. Every institution and industrial organization constantly faces personnel problems because some personalities do not blend well with others, producing antagonism and friction at every administrative level. Many brilliant people are failures in life simply because they are unable to work harmoniously with others. For all of these reasons the problems involved in human relationships are so serious that some of the best minds in the world have devoted themselves to their solution.

At the root of all this difficulty lies man's sinful nature. Individual men and women need to be born again and receive a new life which will enable them to be truly unselfish. However, even after people have been saved, they may still have poor attitudes because of indwelling sin. Therefore Paul in Romans 12:14-21 describes proper Christian conduct toward persecutors, toward all fellow men in general, and toward enemies.

I. Toward Persecutors

The demand that believers invoke God's blessing upon persecutors cannot be fulfilled apart from the enabling power of the indwelling Holy Spirit. Paul says,

> Bless them who persecute you; bless, and curse not (Rom. 12:14).

Persecution may be defined as "unjust and malicious treatment, which comes not for the practice of evil, but for doing right." The normal response to such action is a spirit of resentment and a desire for retaliation.

A. *The Natural Attitude Forbidden*

The inclination to "get even" with one who has wronged us lies deeply imbedded in our fallen human nature. Paul, however, not only unequivocally prohibits revengeful action, but even vindictive thoughts when he says, "Curse not." No matter how wrongly a believer in Christ is treated, he is to confess every resulting hateful thought that wells up within him as sin, and then by God's grace show genuine love for his persecutor.

B. *The Spiritual Attitude Enjoined*

Paul declares that we must "bless them who persecute." This means that Christians are sincerely to pray that God may bless those who unjustly and spitefully seek their harm. The Lord Jesus set an example for us when He prayed, "Father, forgive them; for they know not what they do" (Luke 23:34) while men nailed Him to the cross. Stephen manifested this spirit of Christ when, as the stones pummeled against his body, he prayed, "Lord, lay not this sin to their charge" (Acts 7:60).

This Christlike spirit, though contrary to the inclinations of the natural man, is possible for the believer because he is a new creation (II Cor. 5:17), has been united with Christ, and possesses the indwelling Holy Spirit. God has equipped him to believingly appropriate the words of the Lord Jesus,

> Blessed are they who are persecuted for righteousness' sake; for theirs is the kingdom of heaven.
>
> Blessed are ye, when men shall revile you, and persecute you, and shall say all manner of evil against you falsely, for my sake.
>
> Rejoice, and be exceedingly glad; for great is your reward in heaven; for so persecuted they the prophets who were before you (Matt. 5:10-12).

The person who has received Jesus Christ is an heir of eternal glory, whereas his oppressor as a child of wrath is really to be pitied. The believer therefore follows the example of Jesus and of Stephen, praying for the one who abuses him. Many a persecutor has become a follower of the faith he once sought to destroy because he came in contact with Christians who were able to forgive, to love, and even to pray for their bitterest foes. Saul of Tarsus, for example, saw Stephen die and heard his prayer. He could not escape its impact, and Augustine was undoubtedly right when he said, "The church owes Paul to the prayer of Stephen."

Christian friend, what is your attitude toward those who unjustifiably and bitterly seek to harm you? Do you feel hateful and spiteful toward them? If so, you are not manifesting the spirit of Christ. Ask God's help that you may learn to love them sincerely and to pray for them earnestly.

II. TOWARD FELLOW MEN

Turning from his discussion of the believer's relationship to persecutors, Paul now instructs us regarding our attitude toward our fellow men in general. Romans 12:15-18 teaches that our demeanor toward them is to be marked by sympathy, harmony, and humility.

A. Sympathy

The first admonition of this section, "Rejoice with them that do rejoice," may seem easy to fulfill. When people are having a good time, it is quite natural to share in the spirit of the joyful occasion. This command, however, does not have in view the general merriment of a group of people at a party, but specifically tells us to rejoice when others are especially favored by God, as if the good fortune had been our own. This is sometimes difficult because of our natural proclivity to jealousy and envy, hatred and malice. Chrysostom, one of the early church fathers, said, "It requires more of a high Christian temper to rejoice with them that do rejoice than to weep with them that weep. For this nature itself fulfills perfectly; and there is none so hardhearted as not to weep over him that is in calamity; but the other requires a very noble soul so as not only to keep from envying, but even to feel pleasure with the person who is in esteem." Sincerely congratulating another on his success, especially when it involves disappointment to us, is not easy, but is definitely our Christian duty.

The next directive, that we are to "weep with them that weep" (Rom. 12:15), enjoins us to sympathize with others when they suffer, hoping that we can help the afflicted ones. Certainly we must never rejoice at the calamities of others, and, sad to say, Chrysostom in his otherwise excellent statement was wrong when he said, "There is none so hardhearted as not to weep over him that is in calamity." Really, few people are deeply moved at the plight of those who suffer and sorrow, and some actually are happy when they see certain folk in desperate straits. Moreover, some say they are willing to give money or offer help, but declare their refusal to become emotionally involved. This is decidedly not a proper Christian spirit. Believers do not obey their Master unless they totally share the joys and sorrows of others. Every Christian may well examine his own heart as he contemplates the injunction, "Rejoice with them that do rejoice, and weep with them that weep."

B. *Harmony*

The apostle continues by entreating believers to "be of the same mind one toward another" (Rom. 12:16). Christians should have a warm reciprocal regard for one another because of their common love for Christ, their joint hope in Him, and their mutual desire for His glory. We who know Him should often meditate upon the marvelous oneness of those who are in Christ, emphasizing the many points of agreement rather than the minor differences. A serious consideration of this unity would do a great deal to promote harmony among the followers of the Lord Jesus.

In addition to fostering this peaceable attitude in relation to believers, the Christian is to display an amicable spirit to the world in general. His conduct should commend itself to unsaved men. This is what Paul means when he declares,

> Recompense to no man evil for evil. Provide things honest in the sight of all men (Rom. 12:17).

The common grace of God enables even unbelievers to recognize and approve honest and honorable deportment. When Christians are cruel, dishonest, or impure, they bring reproach upon the name of Christ, and sometimes are put to shame by the conduct of unsaved people. True, godly living will provoke some persecutors to increased hostility, but it will also be the means of promoting a feeling of good will among many who do not know Jesus Christ. When believers live uprightly, some will be attracted to the Savior.

Paul, however, does not suggest that consistent living on the part of Christians will win all men to Christ, nor does he say that it will enable believers to enjoy a peaceful relationship with everyone. Therefore, he says,

> If it be possible, as much as lieth in you, live peaceably with all men (Rom. 12:18).

The expression "if it be possible" indicates that Christians cannot always be at peace with all men. Evil people hate the truth, and sometimes vent their wrath upon those whose godly conduct makes them uncomfortable. Furthermore, there are times when truth, right, and duty demand that we resist certain things. Believers are never to seek a peaceful relationship at the expense of truth and righteousness. One of the older commentaries on Romans makes this observation: "By the side of speaking the *truth in love* must ever stand *loving in truth.*" James declares, "The wisdom that is from above is *first* pure, *then* peaceable" (Jas. 3:17). Paul's phrase, "as much as lieth in you," suggests that whenever collisions occur, the provocation must have come from the side of the unsaved. Though believers are never to violate principles of truth, integrity, and justice, they also must not allow their own personal desires to be the cause for discord. This is what our Lord had in mind when He said,

> But I say unto you that ye resist not evil, but whosoever shall smite thee on thy right cheek, turn to him the other also (Matt. 5:39).

If we must oppose, let it always be for principle, not for our own selfish interests. To love one's neighbor as oneself, seeking his highest welfare, may sometimes require a determined stand against sin, even when it evokes displeasure and gives rise to conflict. However, we must be certain that we do not live by the carnal motto, "No one treads on me unpunished!" In our personal relationships, we must be "peace-lovers," and must bend every effort to be "peacemakers" when it can be done without sacrifice of principle.

C. Humility

Another admonition of this section is an appeal for humility.

> . . . Mind not high things, but condescend to men of low estate. Be not wise in your own conceits (Rom. 12:16).

The phrase which the King James Version renders "men of low estate" in the Greek is simply "the lowly." Expositors are divided as to whether this is a reference to persons or things. Many see in these words an exhortation to take a real interest in ordinary people, to associate freely with lowly and humble folk. Others teach that Paul here requires believers to be content, even when called upon to fill a position considered unimportant. In either case, whether "the lowly" relates to persons or things, this is a demand that Christians avoid all pride and snobbishness, that they be free from vain ambition, grasping for rank and honor. As they relate to others in the Church and in the world, believers must never seek self-exaltation at the expense of those about them. The child of God should be a person with energy, determination, and a desire to be successful in that which he undertakes. However, he should never seek a position in order that he may satisfy his selfish pride or lord it over others.

III. Toward Enemies

The closing directives of Romans 12 set forth the Christian's relationship toward his enemies.

> Dearly beloved, avenge not yourselves but, rather, give place unto wrath; for it is written, Vengeance is mine; I will repay, saith the Lord.
> Therefore, if thine enemy hunger, feed him, if he thirst, give him drink; for in so doing thou shalt heap coals of fire on his head.
> Be not overcome by evil, but overcome evil with good (Rom. 12:19-21).

A distinction can be made between a persecutor and an enemy. The former engages in vicious action against the Christian because he hates the Gospel. The enemy of a believer, on the other hand, may be a wrongdoer who practices dishonesty and cruelty to gratify certain selfish ends, or he may be motivated by personal dislike. The apostle forbids personal acts of revenge, and demands positive deeds of mercy toward all such enemies.

A. *Acts of Vengeance Prohibited*

Even as Paul had exhorted Christians to refrain from retaliatory action or vindictive thoughts toward persecutors, so he commands them to shun all avenging reprisals upon their adversaries. Christians are never to take the law into their own hands, returning evil for evil, or wreaking their vengeance upon others. Instead, they are to "give place unto wrath."

The "wrath" in view here is undoubtedly the "wrath of God." Some interpreters have looked upon this statement as having reference to the judicial penalty exacted by the State, believing that Paul enjoins Christians to let the proper governmental authority administer justice. They point to Romans 13:4 where Paul calls civil government "the minister of God, an avenger to

execute wrath upon him that doeth evil." However, while it is
true that government punishes wrongdoers by divine mandate, the
reference here is to the fact that God will ultimately administer
perfect justice. This is clear from Paul's quotation of Deuteronomy 32:35, "Vengeance is mine; I will repay, saith the Lord."
God alone possesses infinte knowledge of the conditions, the
motives, and the actual result of every wrong deed. He only is
qualified to ultimately recompense all evil. The believer therefore neither seeks personal vengeance nor becomes frustrated
when the State does not administer absolute justice. The way of
faith is to recognize that God is the final Judge, and to leave the
execution of retribution to Him.

B. *Acts of Mercy Commanded*

With this assurance the believer is able to fulfill the next admonition, a demand for ennobling and merciful action.

> Therefore, if thine enemy hunger, feed him; if he thirst,
> give him drink; for in so doing thou shalt heap coals of fire on
> his head (Rom. 12:20).

The spirit that God expects Christians to display toward persecutors as demanded in the words, "Bless them who persecute you;
bless, and curse not" (Rom. 12:14), is now required in relation
to enemies or wrongdoers. Believers are to perform deeds of
mercy to their enemies — feeding them and giving them drink.

The purpose of these kind acts is stated, "for in so doing
thou shalt heap coals of fire on his head." This does not mean
that Christians are to show kindness to an enemy in order that
God's wrath upon him might be more severe. This would be a
malicious motive, displaying an attitude completely contrary to
the spirit of Christian love. The figure of heaping burning em-
bers on the head of the unsaved through kindness means that
our enemies will blush with shame or remorse at such unexpected
treatment. We are therefore to be kind to our enemies, for this
may lead them to repentance. The best way to destroy an enemy is to turn him into a friend through loving deeds.

The concluding words of Romans 12, "Be not overcome by
evil, but overcome evil with good," are an affirmation of the believer's pathway to victory over evil. The Christian life, though
consisting of some prohibitions, some negatives, is not complete
without positive action. Believers will triumph over evil when
they pray for their persecutors, when they become actively in-

volved with others in joy and sorrow, seek harmony, manifest humility, and do good to their enemies. They are overcome by evil every time they stoop to hatred or vengeance. Evil can never be conquered by evil. If hatred is met with more hatred, it is only increased. The only effective antidote is love. Therefore, though Christians know that true peace and harmony will not be attained until the Prince of Peace returns, they are able to manifest the spirit of Christ in their contacts with those about them. In the name of Jesus Christ encouraging smiles should be given, kind words spoken, loving deeds performed. Christian friend, are you manifesting this transformed life in all your relationships?

22

The Christian's Citizenship

The Christian's relationship to civil government is a life-and-death issue in many parts of the world, especially where people live under totalitarian and openly anti-Christian regimes. Therefore, the teaching of Romans 13 is most relevant to our age, for it is concerned with problems encountered by both the early Christians and believers today. In the first place, some followers of Christ assumed that because their citizenship was in Heaven (Phil. 3:20) they were free from obligation to their government. Secondly, Christians were often maltreated by civil authorities, and might have been inclined to feel that these injustices disqualified the State from the right of demanding respect and submission.

To counteract these errors Paul discusses the citizenship of the transformed life — its recognition of civil authority, and its consideration of fellow citizens.

I. RECOGNITION OF CIVIL AUTHORITY

The apostle begins with a straightforward declaration that believers are to be submissive to governmental control, saying, "Let every soul be subject unto the higher powers." This command is based upon three considerations: the divine origin of government, its ordained function, and its acknowledged necessity.

A. *Its Origin — God*

Believers are to be in obedience to government because "there is no power but of God; the powers that be are ordained of God" (Rom. 13:1). This is a clear statement that God established government, and that the authorities in power fill their respective positions by the will of God. True, evil men sometimes gain leadership through dishonesty or violence, but in the final analysis no person would reach this office unless God permitted

164

him to do so. Ultimately, therefore, all authority is derived from God, and believers are commanded to submit to it.

This is not an unfair or burdensome demand. In fact, Christians find great comfort in realizing that the true Sovereign of this tumultuous and chaotic world is God. Though allowing men a great deal of personal freedom, He continues to maintain absolute control. Daniel, a Hebrew lad imprisoned in the far-off country of Babylon, was greatly strengthened by the conviction that his destiny, and that of the nations of earth, was in God's hands. Standing before the great King Nebuchadnezzar, he declared, "Blessed be the name of God forever and ever; for wisdom and might are his . . . he removeth kings, and setteth up kings" (Dan. 2:20, 21). Nebuchadnezzar, proud monarch that he was, himself later confessed that God "doeth according to his will in the army of heaven, and among the inhabitants of the earth, and none can stay his hand, or say unto him, What doest thou?" (Dan. 4:35). No matter how wicked or oppressive the leaders of a country may be, believers are assured that these evil men are not beyond God's control.

In Romans 13:2 the apostle states two reasons Christians are not to resist civil leaders. First, to rebel against them is to oppose God, for He has ordained them to their positions of power. Secondly, the State will punish those who refuse to submit to its authority.

> Whosoever, therefore, resisteth the power, resisteth the ordinance of God; and they that resist shall receive to themselves judgment (Rom. 13:2).

The principle is established that resistance to government constitutes opposition to God.

B. *Its Function — to Promote Righteousness*

But there is another reason Christians should submit to rulers. They are instruments in God's hands to advance the cause of righteousness. Paul says,

> For rulers are not a terror to good works, but to the evil. Wilt thou, then, not be afraid of the power? Do that which is good, and thou shalt have praise of the same.
> For he is the minister of God to thee for good. But if thou do that which is evil, be afraid; for he beareth not the sword in vain; for he is the minister of God, an avenger to execute wrath upon him that doeth evil (Rom. 13:3, 4).

The State normally exerts a restraining influence upon evil men, and commends those citizens who do what is right. In a general sense this has been true throughout history. True, some leaders of nations are godless, and actually hate the Gospel. Furthermore, even in lands where the authorities are favorable to religious freedom, a great deal of dishonesty may be found among political leaders and judges. Normally, however, even under unsaved and corrupt leaders, the civil authorities punish lawbreakers and reward those who conduct themselves in an honorable manner. Even immoral men know that a nation cannot be strong without law enforcement: they recognize that honesty, industry, and truthfulness are necessary ingredients in a well-ordered society.

The right and duty of government to punish crime is explicitly declared in this passage of Scripture. The ruler is described as a "minister of God," who "beareth not the sword in vain," and who is "an avenger to execute wrath upon him that doeth evil." This means that he is God's agent upon earth to administer divine justice. The State is to punish crime that justice may be satisfied, and to forcibly restrain evil for the prevention of anarchy. Many sentimentalists in our day, thinking that civil authorities should safeguard only the rights of the offender, have no concern that crime receive its proper recompense. This is utterly contrary to the Word of God, which clearly teaches that government is to punish those who do wrong, thus carrying out a function forbidden to Christians in their personal relationships.

We know that perfect righteousness is never attained under the rule of sinful men. Some unscrupulous individuals do not receive the punishment they deserve, while others may be penalized beyond the requirements of justice. Believers in Christ, however, must maintain a submissive spirit to their government, obey its laws, and pray for its leaders. They need not be unduly concerned when they see certain injustices uncorrected, for they have the absolute assurance that God will right all wrongs when He holds His final judgment.

C. *Its Necessity — Acknowledged by Conscience*

Christians are to be in subjection to government not only because they know punishment follows disobedience, but also because they approve the efforts of political leaders to promote righteousness.

> Wherefore, ye must needs be subject, not only for wrath but also for conscience' sake (Rom. 13:5).

We may see many imperfections in our governmental leaders, but we must recognize that ultimately the men in power occupy their respective offices because God has either permissively or actively willed them there. We should be grateful for the measure of orderliness and safety that human government has brought society. Therefore, as obedient citizens, we should cheerfully pay our taxes, willingly obey the ordinances of our land, and maintain a respectful spirit toward the men who are in authority.

> For, for this cause pay ye tribute also; for they are God's ministers, attending continually upon this very thing.
> Render, therefore, to all their dues: tribute to whom tribute is due; custom to whom custom; fear to whom fear; honor to whom honor (Rom. 13:6, 7).

D. *Its Qualified Limitation — the Christian's Conscience*

Paul's appeal to the believer's conscience brings to mind a problem the apostle does not discuss. What should be the Christian's course of action when his moral nature cannot help but revolt against a ruthless totalitarian regime, or a government that seems to be hopelessly corrupt? Certainly Paul would agree that Peter and John were right when they rejected the evil demands of magistrates, saying, "We ought to obey God rather than men" (Acts 5:29). The believer cannot obey men when to do so would clearly make him disobedient to God. However, following the example of the apostles, he should obey civil authority whenever possible, and when he cannot comply with its demands without violating his Christian conscience, he should be prepared to submit to the punishment the State requires. Even then he will believe that imperfect government is better than none at all.

This general rule of submission does not preclude the possibility that God may lead certain individual Christians to take part in overthrowing an evil system to set up a new government. Furthermore, some church leaders, though obeying every ordinance that they can fulfill in good conscience, may be led to proclaim Biblical principles showing their government to be wrong in many of its precepts and practices. Such men will run the risk of arrest, imprisonment, even death; but they will make a tremendous impact for righteousness. On one hand, therefore, believers in a country dominated by ungodly men can follow Paul's exhortation to be law-abiding citizens. On the other hand, having been instructed regarding the evils of the existing system, they will pray

for the establishment of a new regime which will promote liberty
and justice, and produce a climate favorable to the Gospel. The
same moral consciousness in the believer which approves even a
poor government as better than anarchy will direct him in time
of revolution to give allegiance to those leaders who have the
greatest interest of mankind at heart.

II. Consideration of Fellow Citizens

Having commanded believers concerning their relationship to
civil authorities, the apostle now turns to the subject of the Christian's responsibility to the society in which he lives. The believer's duties to those about him may be summarized as operating
under the driving force of two dynamic elements in his life —
the law of love and the principle of urgency.

A. *The Law of Love*

The apostle begins his discussion of the Christian's duty to
his fellow citizens by declaring that his only debt should be that
of love.

> Owe no man any thing, but to love one another; for he
> that loveth another hath fulfilled the law (Rom. 13:8).

Love is the believer's "immortal debt," the only one he can never
fully discharge, even if he pays on it every day of his life. Paul
says,

> For this, Thou shalt not commit adultery, Thou shalt not kill,
> Thou shalt not steal, Thou shalt not bear false witness, Thou
> shalt not covet; and if there be any other commandment, it is
> briefly comprehended in this saying, namely, Thou shalt love
> thy neighbor as thyself.
> Love worketh no ill to its neighbor; therefore, love is the
> fulfilling of the law (Rom. 13:9, 10).

Christian love is the creative outgoing of one's personality in
concern for others, even enemies, rather than self. The commandments quoted here forbid us to harm our fellow men in
any way. Since true love never injures another, it fulfills the law.

Believers today need this exhortation. The dizzy whirl of life
has engulfed all of us in our own activities and interests, with the
result that genuine compassion for others is seldom found. We
must remind ourselves of the debt of love we are to continue
paying all our lives. Our duty is to show our love for others in

the Christian witness of kind words and helpful deeds. Christian friend, how long has it been since you have shown real concern for someone outside your family or circle of friends?

B. *The Principle of Urgency*

Having appealed to the law of love as a vital force in the believer's life, Paul continues by emphasizing the uncertainty and brevity of time. He says,

> And that, knowing the time, that now it is high time to awake out of sleep; for now is our salvation nearer than when we believed (Rom. 13:11).

The apostle believed in the imminency of the Lord's return, looking for it to occur at any moment. He longed for the day of rapture and resurrection, for it would mean complete deliverance from sin and all its effects. However, he was also aware that no one could predict the day of the Savior's coming, and recognized the critical nature of the times in which he lived. As he wrote this letter to the Roman Christians, he undoubtedly could see on the horizon indications that the ruling empire would soon begin its persecution of believers, and he knew that the restlessness of the Jews would inevitably lead to a revolt and all the consequences of Rome's fury. God had not revealed to Paul the exact significance of these impending events. In any case, whether by reason of the Lord's immediate return or the outbreak of violent persecution, the apostle wanted all Christians to realize the urgency of the time. Therefore, using the figure of day and night or light and darkness he made a fervent appeal for believers to "put on the armor of light."

> The night is far spent, the day is at hand; let us, therefore, cast off the works of darkness, and let us put on the armor of light.
>
> Let us walk honestly, as in the day; not in reveling and drunkenness, not in immorality and wantonness, not in strife and envying (Rom. 13:12, 13).

The Christian's conduct must always be proper, as in the light of day. In view of the lateness of the hour, how can we spend our time in the wicked deeds men perform under the cover of darkness? We are "children of light," daily expecting the Lord Jesus to return and usher us into the land of endless day. If we are to be effective witnesses for Christ to our fellow citizens, we must live uprightly and work diligently.

The words of Romans 13:14 are a beautiful summary of life under the law of love and the principle of urgency.

> But put ye on the Lord Jesus Christ, and make not provision for the flesh, to fulfill its lusts (Rom. 13:14).

We are daily to put on Jesus Christ as we do our clothing. This means that every day we should consciously remind ourselves of our union with Him, read His Word, fellowship with Him in prayer. Doing this we take preventive measures against the outbreak of sin in our lives. We will not make plans for sin — giving it no welcome, and offering it no opportunity. Sin will not be able to ransack our house if we kick it off the doorstep. A life of communion with Christ, of saying yes to Him and a decided no to sin, makes us good citizens and a means of real help to those with whom we come into contact.

In closing, let me remind you that no one can live the Christian life unless he first receives Jesus Christ as his Savior. Therefore, if you have never entered into a personal relationship with Him, you should do so right now. Bow your head in prayer and settle this matter of your soul's salvation. Here is a suggested word of prayer you might offer: "Lord Jesus, I know that I am a sinner and could never save myself. I believe You died for me and shed Your precious blood for my sin, and that You arose again from the dead. I am receiving You now as my Savior, my Lord, my only hope of salvation. Lord, be merciful to me a sinner, and save me according to the promise of Your Word. In Jesus' name. Amen."

If you prayed this and really meant it, you are saved. The Bible says,

> For whosoever shall call upon the name of the Lord shall be saved (Rom. 10:13).

23

Christian Liberty

The believers of the early Church, converted from Judaism and paganism, were faced with the vexing problem of relating their new freedom in Christ to the practical aspects of life in a non-Christian society. Gentile believers had serious doubts about eating meat that had been offered to pagan idols. Jewish converts were concerned with the same problem, but questioned in addition the eating of meat that was ceremonially unclean. They were also puzzled as they contemplated their responsibility in respect to the sabbath days of their former religious life. Just how much freedom could they exercise in relation to these things?

Some believers, like Paul, had no qualms about eating any kind of wholesome food. They made no distinction between more- and less-sacred days, but regarded every day as "holy unto the Lord." Paul termed such people "strong." Believers with reservations about certain foods, and who still felt that some days were holier than others, were called "weak." (In sharp contrast, the false teachers, with whom Paul dealt severely in his epistles to the Galatians and the Colossians, had distorted the Gospel by setting up a schedule of special days to be observed and a list of foods to be refused as mandatory requirements for salvation.) The "weak" brethren recognized salvation as a gift of God received by faith, and did not consider their obedience to certain scruples a means of earning favor with God. Therefore, the tone of Paul's writing here is that of tenderness, tolerance and restraint. He is dealing with differences between true Christians, and is desirous that harmony be achieved. For this reason he sets down a number of principles by which believers are to be directed as they relate to those who differ with them in non-essentials.

I. MUTUAL RESPECT TO BE MAINTAINED

The first guideline calls for believers to show proper respect for sincere Christians who differ with them on matters of conscience.

Because people come to Christ from divergent backgrounds, and since each person possesses his own unique personality, variances in outlook cannot be avoided. However, believers are not to major on these differences. When a new Christian is accepted into the fellowship of the Church, he is not to be harrassed by those who delight in arguing concerning doubtful points or picayune little regulations. Paul says,

> Him that is weak in the faith receive ye, but not to doubtful disputations.
> For one believeth that he may eat all things: another, who is weak, eateth herbs.
> Let not him that eateth despise him that eateth not; and let not him who eateth not judge him that eateth; for God hath received him (Rom. 14:1-3).

The believers in Rome were to show deferential regard toward the sincere convictions of others. The person who felt no obligation to keep the sabbath because he saw every day as dedicated to God, and who had no compunctions about eating meat that was sold in public places, was admonished not to despise the weaker brother unable to disentangle himself from these taboos and customs. On the other hand, the "weaker" brother had no right to pass judgment upon those who, in the area of the non-essentials, took liberties which he himself in good conscience could not do. Each was to recognize the sincerity of the other.

> He that regardeth the day, regardeth it unto the Lord; and he that regardeth not the day, to the Lord he doth not regard it. He that eateth, eateth to the Lord; for he giveth God thanks; and he that eateth not, to the Lord he eateth not, and giveth God thanks (Rom. 14:6).

Both groups were to govern their conduct by what they believed to be the will of God, whether in eating certain foods or in abstaining from them, or by keeping one day more holy than another. Both lived "unto the Lord." The "weak" brother with his fears was just as devoted to Christ as the "strong" believer who apprehended the full liberty of the Gospel. Therefore Paul admonished them to show proper respect for one another's convictions, and we today should give solemn heed to this exhortation. We are to resist the tendency to magnify the differences that exist between us and other true followers of Christ. We should equally esteem all who love the Lord, avoiding an attitude of disdain toward those whose ideas do not square with ours.

II. ULTIMATE RESPONSIBILITY TO BE RECOGNIZED

In addition to manifesting a spirit of high regard for one another, Christians must be conscious that they are responsible to please God, not fellow believers. Therefore, the person who censoriously judges another Christian is guilty of trespassing an area that belongs to the Lord. Verse 4 declares that no one has the right to pass sentence upon another man's servant, and points out that all believers belong to God, to whom they are answerable, and who is able to preserve them. Moreover, believers have been purchased by Jesus Christ, who died and rose again that they might belong to Him in life and death. He is the Lord of life, for as man He lived perfectly throughout His earthly sojourn. He is also the Lord of death, for He conquered it by His resurrection.

> For none of us liveth to himself, and no man dieth to himself.
> For whether we live, we live unto the Lord; and whether we die, we die unto the Lord; whether we live, therefore, or die, we are the Lord's.
> For to this end Christ both died, and rose, and revived, that he might be Lord both of the dead and living (Rom. 14:7-9).

The Lord Jesus is both Master and Owner of those who trust Him, so Paul says,

> But why dost thou judge thy brother? Or why dost thou set at nought thy brother? For we shall all stand before the judgment seat of Christ.
> For it is written, As I live, saith the Lord, every knee shall bow to me, and every tongue shall confess to God.
> So, then, every one of us shall give account of himself to God (Rom. 14:10-12).

We are under divine scrutiny, and therefore we are not the judges but the ones to be judged. How dare we either pass sentence upon or despise our brother? Such action involves presumptuous forgetfulness of two truths: first, that we have not been appointed judges; and, second, that we and the brother we are tempted to judge will alike stand at the tribunal of Christ. If we are constantly aware of our own faults and failings before God, we will not be quick to look with disdain upon another. Christian friend, remember that you must someday give an account of *yourself,* not of someone else; and to *God,* not man.

III. LOVE TO BE PRACTICED

Having warned Christians against despising or passing sentence upon one another, the apostle declares that we are to judge ourselves, searching our own hearts to see that we are manifesting love in our attitude toward other believers.

> Let us not, therefore, judge one another any more; but judge this, rather: that no man put a stumbling block or an occasion to fall in his brother's way (Rom. 14:13).

A person whose life is regulated by Christian love will not continue any activity which hurts his brother, for he is genuinely concerned with the welfare of others.

To further emphasize the primacy of love, the apostle stated ". . . that there is nothing unclean of itself" (Rom. 14:14). The whole legal system came to an end when Christ paid the price for sin and conquered death by resurrection. Paul states further that he was "persuaded by the Lord Jesus " (Rom. 14:14). Therefore he was able to carry his knowledge into practice without violating his conscience. He had no inhibitions in relation to eating meat that was ceremonially unacceptable.

> I know, and am persuaded by the Lord Jesus, that there is nothing unclean of itself . . . (Rom. 14:14).

However, though the apostle felt no inner compulsion to obey the dietary rules of the Hebrew faith, he would not exercise his liberty if it meant offending a sincere believer.

> But if thy brother be grieved with thy food, now walketh thou not in love. Destroy not him with thy food, for whom Christ died (Rom. 14:15).

The Christian who exercises his liberty of conscience to the full, with no regard for the "weaker" brother, can cause a great deal of harm. In fact, he may "destroy" another believer. This strong word, "destroy," underlines the seriousness of the injury that can result. Paul was not implying the possibility of losing salvation through the conduct of a fellow Christian, but declared that the weaker brother's effectiveness as a witness, his assurance of salvation, his confidence in prayer and his peace of heart may be destroyed. Certainly no sincere believer would willfully bring such harm to a brother in Christ.

IV. RIGHTEOUSNESS, PEACE, AND JOY TO BE SOUGHT

Believers need also to recognize that the essence of the Christian life does not consist of mere externals, but uprightness of conduct, peacefulness of attitude and mind, and radiant Christian joy. What you eat, or what day you consider holy, is not of paramount importance.

> Let not then your good be evil spoken of;
> For the kingdom of God is not food and drink, but righteousness, and peace, and joy in the Holy Spirit.
> For he that in these things serveth Christ is acceptable to God, and approved of men (Rom. 14:16-18).

Christian friend, what is the emphasis of *your* life? Are you a fault-finding person, having your own ideas concerning proper foods, modest dress, or acceptable hair styles? Do you severely criticize all who do not conform to your standards? Or, on the other hand, are you basically selfish in your attitude, doing what you recognize you have a right to do without considering the feelings and convictions of others? In either instance you are wrong! Those who spend their time insisting upon their rights or criticizing others do not manifest the spirit of Christ. Examine your own life. Are you showing forth the uprightness of life, the peacefulness of spirit, and the joy of assurance which ought to mark the children of God?

This emphasis leads Paul to affirm that the true believer should be motivated by a sincere desire for harmony and a genuine concern for the welfare of his fellow Christians. Paul says,

> Let us, therefore, follow after the things which make for peace, and things with which one may edify another.
> For food destroy not the work of God . . . (Rom. 14:19, 20).

V. CONSCIENCE TO BE HONORED

There is one more principle to be considered. We are to honor every individual's conscience. God has given each of us an inner faculty by which we may distinguish between good and evil, and through which we are urged to do right and refrain from wrong. Conscience is not an infallible guide because its judgments in part are based upon external influences. Therefore, a person who from childhood was taught to avoid certain foods or keep a special day may be uneasy when he breaks these rules, even after he has intellectually concluded they are not divine mandates. The question is whether he must obey the voice of conscience, or resolutely use the liberty he has.

The apostle answers this question by declaring that a believer must never violate conscience — his own or that of another. The person who is able to eat every kind of wholesome food without inner uneasiness must be careful to show respect for the one unable to do so. Though this "strong" believer is convinced of his right to be free from stipulations regarding food and the keeping of days, he does not parade his privileges and liberties to the detriment of the person with the fearful conscience. He knows the truth of Martin Luther's words, "A Christian man is a most free lord of all, subject to none," but also believes and practices the reformer's next sentence, "A Christian man is a most dutiful servant of all, subject to all." Paul exhorts the "strong" believer,

> It is good neither to eat meat, nor to drink wine, nor anything by which thy brother stumbleth, or is offended, or is made weak.
> Hast thou faith? Have it to thyself before God. Happy is he that condemneth not himself in that thing which he alloweth (Rom. 14:21, 22).

On the other hand, the believer who is unable to live in the full liberty of the Gospel should recognize that his legalistic deeds do not make him more acceptable in God's sight than others. He should seek to appropriate the truth that the essence of the Christian life is righteousness, peace, and joy. However, he should definitely refrain from doing that which his conscience forbids. As long as he has inner doubts about a practice, he should personally refrain from it. Paul says,

> And he that doubteth is condemned if he eat, because he eateth not of faith; for whatever is not of faith is sin (Rom. 14:23).

In summary, followers of Jesus Christ must recognize that variations in some areas of thought are inevitable. You must show proper respect for those who have differing viewpoints on some things. Furthermore, each of you is to recognize that God is the final and ultimate Judge of all men. Therefore you are not to judge others, nor are you to violate your own conscience for the approval of fellow men. Our aim in life is to be well-pleasing to God.

Remember also that you are not to place undue emphasis upon external observances, for you are to be motivated by a spirit of love. Every believer is his brother's keeper, responsible not only for himself, but for all who come into contact with him. But you must also honor your conscience. If your heart tells you something is wrong, you must obey this inner voice. If you do not, you will harm yourself, and scar your own personality.

24

Christian Behavior

Jesus Christ is the supreme example of moral behavior for believers. True, He is far more than a perfect man, and His purpose for coming to earth was not merely to set a pattern for us, but to be our Savior. A genuine believer will accept the great historical doctrines regarding the Son of God — His deity, His virgin birth, His perfect life, His substitutionary death for sinners, His resurrection, His ascension to Heaven, and His literal and visible return. And the primary task of the Christian is to proclaim the good news of salvation to people lost in sin. However, we sometimes seem to forget that Jesus Christ is also our perfect pattern — an example for us to follow. The epistles emphasize this truth in many passages, admonishing Christians to look to Jesus as their ideal and inspiration. The fifteenth chapter of Romans, the topic of our study, holds up the Lord Jesus as our perfect model. We are to be imitators of Him in loving concern for all, in sympathetic understanding of all, and in joyous hope.

I. CHRISTLIKE CONCERN

If we know Christ, we are to please God, not self. Paul says,

> We, then, that are strong ought to bear the infirmities of the weak, and not to please ourselves.
> Let every one of us please his neighbor for his good to edification (Rom. 15:1, 2).

When we are thinking of our fellow believer's welfare, seeking "his good to edification," we will put his spiritual well-being above our own personal desires. We should be happy to give up something we enjoy, even if it is perfectly lawful and proper, to be a real help to a brother in Christ. In so doing, we follow the Lord Jesus as our peerless example.

> For even Christ pleased not himself; but, as it is written, The reproaches of them that reproached thee fell on me (Rom. 15:3).

This quotation from Psalm 69 points out that Jesus endured reproach and insult because of His faithfulness to God. He did not please Himself. He would not have endured this suffering had He not been concerned about obeying His Heavenly Father. He came to do the Father's will. On the eve of His crucifixion the Lord Jesus prayed,

> I have glorified thee on the earth; I have finished the work which thou gavest me to do (John 17:4).

A little later, in the Garden of Gethsemane, our Lord contemplated the bitterness of the cup of suffering He was about to take for the sins of the world. The awfulness of being forsaken by God, of bearing the divine wrath against sin, of dying the accursed death of the cross to take the punishment sinners deserve — these weighed heavily on Him. Yet in His prayer He expressed His total submission to the will of His Heavenly Father.

> . . . Father, if thou be willing, remove this cup from me; nevertheless, not my will, but thine, be done (Luke 22:42).

The Lord Jesus left Heaven's glory to take upon Himself our humanity, enduring pain, abuse, shame, and torture, that He might in obedience to the Father provide salvation for sinful mankind. Since He did all this for us, should we not show similar concern for others? He did not insist upon His rights, and neither should we. Our aim in life should be to do the will of God, putting aside our own selfish desires and interests that our lives may be spiritually helpful to those with whom we come in contact.

II. CHRISTLIKE UNDERSTANDING

In addition to showing loving concern, a Christlike person is characterized by sympathetic understanding of others. This means that we will be able to have a deep love and respect for the person with whom we differ, even though we may not be in perfect agreement in some matters of doctrine. The apostle earnestly desires that this spiritual quality be evident among the saints to whom he is writing.

> Now the God of patience and consolation grant you to be likeminded one toward another according to Christ Jesus,

> That ye may with one mind and one mouth glorify God,
> even the Father of our Lord Jesus Christ (Rom. 15:5, 6).

These words express a desire which is both a prayer to God and an exhortation to men. Paul knows that believers will never be able to experience deep oneness of spirit, enabling them to overlook their petty differences with others, unless they receive the patience and comfort imparted by God through His Word. "That we, through patience and comfort of the scriptures, might have hope" (Rom. 15:4).

Friend, God calls on you to feed your soul upon His Word, drawing from it encouragement and spiritual adequacy to live completely above the envyings and jealousies that so often mar Christian fellowship.

God longs that we "be likeminded one toward another *according to Christ Jesus*." The Lord by precept and example taught us how we should feel and act in relation to all — even those who treat us wrongly. He manifested a sympathetic understanding of His disciples when they showed a weakness of faith, when they slept while they should have been praying, and when they lacked courage to publicly identify themselves with Him in the dreadful hours between Gethsemane and Calvary. He understood their failures, and graciously reassured them after His resurrection. This moral attitude of Christ, this supreme demonstration of self-forgetfulness and compassion, was the basis of Paul's exhortation to the Christians in Philippi, "Let this mind be in you, which was also in Christ Jesus " (Phil. 2:5). We can never do better than to direct the attention of men to the example set by the Lord Jesus when urging them to kindness, unity, and humility.

Fellow believer, how much time do you spend in the Word of God? Do you read its sacred pages and meditate upon its truths until your heart is filled with its comfort, encouragement, and hope? Do you reflect upon the life and death of Jesus Christ your Savior? Do you seriously look upon Him as the pattern for your life? If you do, you will develop a Christlike attitude to others and feel the bond of unity which makes you one with all who love Christ. The result will be the realization of Paul's earnest desire, "That ye may with one mind and one mouth glorify God, even the Father of our Lord Jesus Christ" (Rom. 15:6).

III. CHRISTLIKE INCLUSIVENESS

A third characteristic of Christlike behavior is having a love that is broad in scope, accepting fellow believers regardless of their status in life. The apostle declares that we are to follow the example of Christ.

> Wherefore, receive ye one another, as Christ also received us to the glory of God.
>
> Now I say that Jesus Christ was a minister of the circumcision for the truth of God, to confirm the promises made unto the fathers (Rom. 15:7, 8).

Furthermore, James denounces all favoritism.

> My brethren, have not the faith of our Lord Jesus Christ, the Lord of glory, with respect of persons.
>
> For if there come unto your assembly a man with a gold ring, in fine apparel, and there come in also a poor man in vile raiment,
>
> And ye have respect to him that weareth the fine clothing, and say unto him, Sit thou here in a good place; and say to the poor, Stand thou there, or sit here under my footstool,
>
> Are ye not then partial in yourselves, and are become judges with evil thoughts?
>
> Hearken, my beloved brethren, Hath not God chosen the poor of this world to be rich in faith and heirs of the kingdom which he hath promised to them that love him? (Jas. 2:1-5).

James pictures believers of his day extending undue deference to the rich man who enters a Christian assembly wearing jewelry and gorgeous garments, while telling a shabbily dressed man that he must either stand, or sit on the floor. In so doing, these believers completely ignored the example of Jesus Christ, and wickedly violated the essence of Christian brotherhood, which declares that all, rich and poor alike, are precious to God.

We are often guilty of possessing an unforgiving heart, while preaching equality for all and salvation for the vilest of men. We have a tendency to despise those who have fallen into deep sin. Many of our churches minister only to people in the middle or higher income brackets, and show little concern for the people who live in the inner city or on the other side of the tracks. We ought to reflect upon the greatness of God's love for us, upon His patience and continuing mercy, until we see how unworthy of His love and grace we are. Once we truly understand God's grace as related to our own depravity, we will not find it in our hearts to be disdainful of others.

IV. Christlike Joy and Peace

Having set forth the truth that Christlike conduct involves loving concern and sympathetic understanding, Paul closes this section of his epistle with an indirect prayer which combines invocation and exhortation.

> Now the God of hope fill you with all joy and peace in believing, that ye may abound in hope, through the power of the Holy Spirit (Rom. 15:13).

A believer will experience sweet inner peace and radiate abounding joy when he sincerely seeks to follow the example of Jesus Christ. These qualities are not superficial feelings induced by closing one's eyes to reality. Rather, they stem from the hope God Himself has brought to the hearts of those who trust Him. He is "the God of hope." Looking back in faith, the believer sees the cross of Christ, His resurrection, His ascension to Heaven, and the coming of the Holy Spirit on the day of Pentecost. Looking forward, this same faith centers upon the glorious return of the Lord Jesus, and the eternal bliss that awaits those who belong to Him.

> Beloved, now are we the children of God, and it doth not yet appear what we shall be, but we know that, when he shall appear, we shall be like him; for we shall see him as he is (I John 3:2).

Even the Lord Jesus, the Son of God, was strengthened as He anticipated the effect of the cross. The writer of Hebrews tells us,

> . . . who for the joy that was set before him endured the cross, despising the shame, and is set down at the right hand of the throne of God (Heb. 12:2).

The "joy that was set before him" was the expectation of sharing glory with all those who would be redeemed by His death.

Furthermore, the unruffled peace and equanimity manifested by Christ throughout His earthly ministry, especially apparent in those last hours, were also closely associated with hope. In the upper room with His disciples on the eve of His crucifixion, Christ was perfectly composed as He projected Himself forward beyond the cross to the glory of eternity. With quiet confidence He said, "Father, I will that they also, whom thou hast given me, be with me where I am, that they may behold my glory, which thou hast given me; for thou lovest me before the foundation of the world" (John 17:24). Our Lord's radiant joy and unwavering peace stemmed from His implicit faith and confident hope.

Christian friend, God has given you a glorious prospect. The purpose of the Lord's death and resurrection was to provide salvation, making possible for you an eternity in Heaven. Consider the glory that awaits you. Reflect upon what it will be like to see the Lord Jesus face to face. Think of the great company who have gone before, and of the fact that you will be in their midst. This is the true Christian hope, and the life of the person to whom it is real will be characterized by joy and peace. Not only that, your hope will become increasingly precious, your vision of glory more bright, and the power of God more evident as you travel the road that leads to Heaven.

25

A Man of God

When reading the epistles of Paul, we must remember that they are letters to churches or individuals, not textbooks on theology. While expressing the most profound theological truths of the Christian faith, they have the warmth of a letter to a friend, revealing the kind of person Paul was. In them we see the apostle as intense, strong, and courageous, yet thoroughly human, possessing a keen sense of humor and an affectionate regard for his co-workers. These qualities of his character are clearly reflected in the warm, personal conclusion of his epistle to the Romans. We see this man of God as he speaks of his manifold task, tells his cherished plans, greets his beloved friends, and finally breaks forth in a jubilant doxology of praise.

I. HIS MANIFOLD TASK

Responding to a special call of God to be His chosen apostle to the Gentiles, Paul became the greatest missionary of the Church, planting many local assemblies of believers. He was responsible for their spiritual nurture, and since it was impossible for him to revisit all of them in person he wrote many letters. The Holy Spirit, who had revealed distinctive truths to this special apostle, also guided him in writing these epistles, and they have become an important part of the inerrant Scriptures. Thus Paul was highly honored by God, was the greatest of the apostles, and authored more of the New Testament than any other man. In spite of all this exaltation, however, Paul never became proud. When on occasion it was necessary for him to vindicate his apostleship, he always did so in a spirit of humility and reluctance. These characteristics stand out clearly in Romans 15:14-21 where he exercises his role as a tactful teacher, asserts his apostolic appointment, and speaks of himself as a pioneer missionary.

A. *A Tactful Teacher*

Though Paul undoubtedly knew God had given him more revelation than any other apostle, he never paraded his superiority. He was always kind, did not angrily rebuke God's children, nor unnecessarily assert his authority. He genuinely loved the people to whom he ministered, and as he closed his epistle to the Romans he was hopeful that they would accept his admonition in the proper spirit. Therefore, he began by commending them, acknowledging both their goodness of heart and their fullness of Christian understanding.

> And I myself also am persuaded of you, my brethren, that ye also are full of goodness, filled with all knowledge, able also to admonish one another (Rom. 15:14).

He goes on to tell them that he wrote to refresh their memories, and, though it might seem he had written somewhat boldly, he had dealt only with those issues his special grace as an apostle authorized him to handle. We might paraphrase this section as follows: "I know there is much which you could teach me about the Christian life, but my apostleship requires that I remind you of certain important truths."

> Nevertheless, brethren, I have written the more boldly unto you in some sort, as putting you in mind, because of the grace that is given to me of God (Rom. 15:15).

Every person who exercises leadership in the Church should learn from this dedicated apostle. Many of the disruptions that take place in local assemblies could be avoided if every leader manifested the humility, kindness and tact exemplified by this man of God.

B. *An Appointed Apostle*

In verses 16 through 18 Paul declares that he has been appointed the apostle to the Gentiles, that he proclaims the Gospel as a priestly service, and that his Gentile converts are the offerings he presents to God.

> That I should be the minister of Jesus Christ to the Gentiles, ministering the gospel of God, that the offering up of the Gentiles might be acceptable, being sanctified by the Holy Spirit (Rom. 15:16).

The three Greek words translated "minister," "ministering," and "offering," are all sacrificial terms. Paul is saying that no one has a right to reject these Gentile believers, for they were "sanctified by the Holy Spirit."

Whatever glorying the apostle may do is "through Jesus Christ" (verse 17). He declares that the winning of the Gentiles is not his work, but "through mighty signs and wonders, by the power of the Spirit of God" (Rom. 15:19). With no trace of self-exaltation but with an earnest desire to glorify Christ, Paul affirms the genuineness of his apostleship.

C. A Pioneer Missionary

The apostle's greatest delight was to proclaim the Gospel in areas where churches did not exist.

> Yea, so have I strived to preach the gospel, not where Christ was named, lest I should build upon another man's foundation (Rom. 15:20).

How thankful we should be for this great missionary pioneer who founded churches throughout the Roman Empire, and for the many others with the same burden who have carried on his task! David Livingstone is an example. He felt compelled to apply for missionary service in Africa, and when he got there was haunted by the smoke of a thousand villages which he saw in the distance. He could not do other than make Christ known to those who sat in darkness, and he finally died at his task. Though he and some others like him have become famous, most of these stalwart missionary pioneers lived and died in obscurity. Only eternity will reveal the fruit of their sacrifice and devotion.

Christian friend, the world still desperately needs the Gospel, and many areas do not contain one Bible-preaching church. God still calls young people to serve Him, that His salvation might be proclaimed in these places. You may be one whom God is calling to such a field of labor. He places upon all of us the responsibility to be His witness wherever we are, to tell those around us the wonderful story of Jesus. In this way, each of us can be a man of God, or a woman of God. What higher title could we bear!

II. HIS CHERISHED PLANS

Paul, like almost everyone else, had plans for the future. He had never visited the church at Rome, and hoped to stop there on his way to Spain. However, he was intending an immediate trip to Jerusalem.

A. *His Immediate Trip to Jerusalem*

The apostle felt an urgent need to present the saints in Jerusalem a love gift from a number of the Gentile churches he had founded. He says,

> But now I go unto Jerusalem to minister unto the saints.
> For it hath pleased them of Macedonia and Achaia to make a certain contribution for the poor saints who are at Jerusalem (Rom. 15:25, 26).

Apparently many of the people who had turned from Judaism to Christ had lost their jobs and had been ostracized from their families. Paul had reminded the Gentile believers that salvation came through Israel, and told them that they had a moral obligation to help these Jewish believers who were enduring hardships because of their faith in Christ.

> . . . For if the Gentiles have been made partakers of their spiritual things, their duty is also to minister unto them in carnal things (Rom. 15:27).

Paul wished to deliver the gift personally that he might make sure the money was properly distributed, and also to "seal" the gift as a blessing from God (Rom. 15:28).

Knowing that danger awaited him in Jerusalem, Paul called upon the believers in Rome to beseech the throne of God in intercessory prayer on his behalf.

> Now I beseech you, brethren, . . . that ye strive together with me in your prayers to God for me:
> That I may be delivered from them that do not believe in Judaea . . . (Rom. 15:30, 31).

The book of Acts, chapter 21, shows how the Holy Spirit, first through disciples at Tyre and then through a prophet named Agabus, warned Paul that he would be imprisoned if he carried out his plan. The apostle, however, expressed his sincere conviction that it was God's will for him to go to Jerusalem, and also declared that he was prepared to endure whatever might come his way. From the history recorded in the book of Acts, we know that Paul was arrested, imprisoned, and that later he went to Rome bound in chains.

B. *A Future Journey to Spain*

Paul's long-range plans included a missionary tour to Spain. Undoubtedly he was challenged by the fact that Spain was strategically of great importance, being at the western end of Europe, the outward limits of the civilized world of his day. Paul believed that if he could go there with the Gospel, the message of salvation would soon permeate the entire continent and have worldwide results. No one on earth today knows whether or not Paul ever reached this country. Most Bible students believe that after Paul's arrest and first detention in Rome he was released for a short time, but then imprisoned again. It may be that he did indeed preach in Spain, but this cannot be said with any degree of certainty.

Paul did not foresee, as he wrote this letter to Rome, how things would work out. He knew danger awaited him in Jerusalem, but did not know that he would finally go to Rome as a prisoner in chains. However, in all of his disappointments he was submissive to the will of God. The man who had endured ridicule, hatred, beatings, and shipwreck was ready for whatever might be his portion, confident that nothing could ever separate him from the love of God. We often say, "Man proposes, but God disposes." How true! From Paul, a man who perhaps above all others deserved the appellation "A man of God," we learn that the most devoted Christian may make his plans, but he must always say, "Not my will, but thine be done."

III. His FRIENDS

Though Paul possessed a brilliant mind capable of keen insight and devastating logic, and though he was a devoted person who spent a great deal of time in reading, meditations, and prayer, he always retained a great delight in fellowshiping with his friends and co-workers. This is evident in Romans 16, where he first presents a kindly introduction of Phoebe, who would be delivering his letter, then sends his greetings to a group of people, solemnly warns them, and relays salutations from mutual friends. Only a man genuinely interested in people would have given so much time to these personal remarks.

Paul specifically greets twenty-eight different individuals. The fact that he had so many friends in a city he had never visited gives us an index to the kind of man he was. Christian people loved him dearly. The ones mentioned here undoubtedly lived in Rome, but had met Paul in some other place. Aquila and

Priscilla had risked their lives for him (verses 3, 4), and the mother of a man named Rufus (verse 13) must have treated the apostle as if he were her son. The apostle greatly appreciated these friends, longed to speak to them personally, and could not refrain from sending them his cordial greetings. Throughout his entire ministry he actively mixed with people, showing them love, compassion, and tender regard.

In today's busy world, the value of Christian fellowship is sometimes overlooked by God's people. This is indeed a spiritual tragedy. When believers share their problems and experiences, they are strengthened and uplifted. Many people in great pain or sorrow have testified that the kind words, the greetings and the prayers of fellow Christians were a pillar of strength in the time of crisis. Believers should cultivate fellowship with one another. It will add delight to the Christian experience in times when all goes well, and will be a means in God's hands to give strength and support in the hour of need. The prophet Malachi spoke of a situation in which a godless society with its anti-God conversation drove believers together for mutual encouragement and unified witness.

> Then they that feared the LORD spoke often one to another; and the LORD hearkened, and heard it, and a book of remembrance was written before him for them that feared the LORD. and that thought upon his name (Mal. 3:16).

B. *His Warning*

Paul found it difficult to bring this letter to a close, and, after sending his greetings to these special friends, he made one last appeal that they keep themselves from every evil influence.

> Now I beseech you, brethren, mark them who cause divisions and offenses contrary to the doctrine which ye have learned; and avoid them.
> For they that are such serve not our Lord Jesus Christ but their own body, and by good works and fair speeches deceive the hearts of the innocent (Rom. 16:17, 18).

False teachers were seeking to disrupt Christian fellowship, saying that freedom from law meant to live in licentiousness. They were creating divisions among the saints and causing some to fall into sin. Paul, his great heart filled with love and concern for the believers in Rome, felt compelled to warn them. He was confident that these Roman believers would know how to deal with such false teachers, and was assured that God would win the final victory over Satan, but nevertheless thought this word of loving admonition to be needful.

> For your obedience is come abroad unto all men. I am glad, therefore, on your behalf; but yet I would have you wise unto that which is good, and simple concerning evil.
> And the God of peace shall bruise Satan under your feet shortly. The grace of our Lord Jesus Christ be with you. Amen. (Rom. 16:19, 20).

Every Christian must be on guard at all times against the hypocrites who, behind a façade of pious and religious words, lead people astray. If you as a believer see such a person operating within your church, you have a solemn duty to issue an immediate warning. Your failure to do so might result in the loss of the church's testimony in the community, or in some new Christian's falling into serious doctrinal error or sin. Paul, as a man of God, never hesitated to expose error, and neither should you.

IV. His Jubilant Doxology

The glowing doxology which closes the book of Romans is both a summary of the message Paul preached and a commentary on the kind of man he was.

> Now to him that is of power to establish you according to my gospel, and the preaching of Jesus Christ, according to the revelation of the mystery, which was kept secret since the world began,
> But now is made manifest, and by the scriptures of the prophets, according to the commandment of the everlasting God, made known to all nations for the obedience of faith:
> To God, only wise, be glory through Jesus Christ forever. Amen (Rom. 16:25-27).

A. *Power to Stand*

The Gospel is first of all a message by which God makes men able to stand firm — "Now to him that is of power to establish you according to my gospel." Only God's power keeps a man safe and enables him to stand against the assaults of temptation and the shocks of life's difficult circumstances. The power of God revealed in Jesus Christ enabled Paul to be victorious through all the painful and disappointing experiences he was called to endure. Though troubled on every side, he was not distressed; though often perplexed, he did not despair; though he was bitterly persecuted, he knew God had never forsaken him; though he was often cast down, he was never destroyed. (See II Cor. 4:8, 9.)

B. *Explanation of History*

In this doxology Paul also expressed his firm confidence that the Gospel is the key to the understanding of all history. God's glorious salvation through Christ was seen in shadow through the ages from creation until the incarnation, but with His entrance into the world it was clearly revealed. This is what Paul means when he speaks of the "revelation of the mystery" which "now is made manifest, and by the scriptures of the prophets, according to the commandment of the everlasting God, made known to all nations." Paul saw Jesus Christ as the pivot-point of history. He looked upon all the ages before Christ as pointing to the Son of God, and all subsequent history as flowing from Him. He also rejoiced in the fact that this Gospel is offered to all men in every nation. With such a philosophy of history, Paul could live above circumstances, could rejoice in hope, even in the darkness of midnight. Assured of God's infinite holiness, wisdom, power, and love, he closed this letter with a note of praise, "To God, only wise, be glory through Jesus Christ forever. Amen."

From the book of Acts and Paul's later epistles we know that this man of God experienced almost indescribable hardships soon after he had written these words. However, he faced them with courage as a Christian hero, bearing a good witness for his Savior. Shortly before his death, sitting on the damp, dirty floor of the Mamertine Prison, suffering almost unbearable loneliness, chilled to the very bone, and realizing that death was near, this noble soldier of Christ could write to Timothy,

> I have fought a good fight, I have finished my course, I have kept the faith;
> Henceforth there is laid up for me a crown of righteousness, which the Lord, the righteous judge, shall give me at that day; and not to me only, but unto all them also that love his appearing (II Tim. 4:7, 8).

CONCLUSION

Dear reader, earthly life is uncertain and brief. It often consists of a great deal of heartbreak, sorrow, and suffering. These facts, however, should not depress the one who knows Christ. God does not intend this earthly scene to be our eternal abode. He allows us a short probationary period here during which we prepare for our eternal abiding place. The important matter is not the degree of success we have achieved or the amount of temporal pleasure we have squeezed out of life, but how we have built for eternity. If you, like the apostle Paul, sincerely seek to do the will of God, cheerfully submit to His disciplines, and through the power of the indwelling Christ display the fruit of the Spirit — love, joy, peace, long-suffering, gentleness, goodness, faith, meekness, temperance — the termination of life upon earth will hold no terrors for you. You will be able to live in the joyous expectancy of the imminent return of Jesus Christ to take you to himself, or, if the Lord tarries, you have the assurance that your death will be immediate entrance into glory.

To you who do not know Christ as your Savior, let me remind you that you will never find true happiness if you bypass Jesus Christ. Without Him, life has no meaning and no glorious purpose or destiny. You are a slave of sin, guilty in God's sight, under condemnation, and on your way to a dark and hopeless eternity. Turn to Jesus Christ today, believing that golden verse of the Bible,

> For God so loved the world, that he gave his only begotten Son, that whosoever believeth in him should not perish, but have everlasting life (John 3:16).

Why not bow your heard in prayer and settle this matter of your soul's salvation? Do it now!

Property of
First Assembly of God
Santa Barbara, California

The WORLD on TRIAL

STUDIES IN ROMANS

Richard W. DeHaan

A devotional commentary which proceeds section-by-section through the book of Romans.

Here Richard DeHaan, famed teacher of the Radio Bible Class, approaches the book of Romans from a distinctly practical point of view and relates its teachings to many of today's issues in the Christian life.

Included are chapters on:
Trial of Immoral Pagan
Trial of Self-righteous Moralists
Trial of Proud Religionists
God's Righteousness Vindicated
Becoming Right With God
From Marooned to Redemption
From Death to Resurrection
From Sin's Tyranny to God's Dominion
Freedom From Law
The Struggle With Sin
Victory and Sonship
Suffering and Glory
The Shout of Triumph

[*continued on back flap*]

The World on Trial
No. 6397 Zondervan